Permission to Flourish

Cultivating Courage, Embracing Change

Elisa James

Foreward

Copyright ©2024
All rights reserved.

Cover art, book design, and formatting by The Time Queen Co., Ltd.

No part of this book may be used or reproduced in any manner whatsoever without written permission by the author.

This book represents the collective effort of multiple co-authors, each sharing their personal viewpoints and experiences. It is a reflection of diverse perspectives, transcending differences in religion, spiritual beliefs, and viewpoints. Our intention is to bring together a mosaic of voices, fostering a sense of unity and expression without judgment. Please understand that the content within these pages is meant for exploration and understanding, and does not necessarily reflect any universal truths or consensus among the co-authors. We encourage readers to approach this book with an open heart and appreciation for the richness of human diversity.

All contributors to this work have duly consented to the use of their personal data, facts, recollections, memories, and / or experiences found herein. They are aware that the end and intended result was mass production and publication in connection with this work. As such, they have agreed without equivocation or caveat to indemnify, defend, and hold harmless the collaborator and publisher of this material, along with their affiliates, officers, directors, employees, and agents from any and all claims, damages, expenses, and liabilities arising out of or in connection with the use of such personal data, facts, recollections, memories, and experiences, including any claims of infringement of intellectual property rights or violation of privacy rights.

Tables of Contents

Foreword
Elisa James — 1

Chapter 1: **The Strongest Mantra – KAYA MO!** — 4
Ailien Tulio

Chapter 2: **The Courage to Persevere and Change** — 12
Stephanie Sullivan

Chapter 3: **Facing the Existential Crisis** — 23
Melanie Naumann

Chapter 4: **Bonding with the Inner Child** — 32
Leyla Mesic

Chapter 5: **When the Time is Right** — 41
Shaira Beth Dillena

Chapter 6: **Walking Away from Success** — 50
Jai Cornell

Chapter 7: **Following Your Heart** — 58
Leska Prokopets

Chapter 8: **The Wave of life** — 67
Aimee Kaopua-Hersey

Chapter 9: **Flip the Script** 75
Issabele Popescu

Chapter 10: **Embracing Change & Adversity for a Better Life** 84
Chantelle Lynch

Chapter 11: **Beauty Can Come from Brokenness** 94
Rachel Hewitt

Chapter 12: **The Unexpected Path to Self-Discovery** 105
Jennifer Lee

Chapter 13: **HIStory** 117
Jay C. Denis

Chapter 14: **Building Unwavering Self-Belief** 128
Stephanie Sullivan

Epilogue 138

Foreword

Elisa James Th.M., M.Mus

As a featured author in the previous two volumes of our book series Permission to Flourish, I have witnessed firsthand the incredible resilience of the human spirit as shared so bravely by my co-authors in the first two books. Our third book continues in the same vein, highlighting the challenges we face and the resilience we develop as we build the inner strength required to overcome life's unexpected challenges. I feel honored as a fellow author to have been asked to write this forward, especially since life has indeed thrown me more than my fair share of curve balls. Perhaps I wouldn't be the person I am today without the challenges I've had to face head-on. Challenges and adversity can shape us in both positive and negative ways. It can both break us down and simultaneously transform us into better human beings. That is, if you adopt the right mindset to look at the enriching life lessons that are sometimes hidden in, what seems like at the time, the depths of despair.

Permission to Flourish: Cultivating Courage, Embracing Change is a testament to the durability of the human spirit. Each author in this third book has personally faced, at times, unfathomable hardships in their lives, surviving extremely tragic and traumatic experiences in some cases. These experiences could easily break a person, whether it's personal trauma, professional setbacks, or internal struggles they may be grappling with. Yet, through tenacity, determination, and an unwavering belief in a better future, they have not only transformed their own lives but are now guiding their clients to do the same.

Personally, I learned at a very young age that with grit and perseverance I could turn some of the biggest obstacles I faced into stepping stones to help me fully grow into my potential. My personal goal was to find my authentic voice of confident self-expression, and as I navigated that difficult and arduous task as a shy, insecure youngster, I eventually found my voice of leadership and authority as well. Similar to the authors in this book, I too have faced moments in my life that required me to adopt a complete mindset shift, a commitment to learning new and difficult skills, and garner a deeper understanding of who I really wanted to become.

What makes this book series truly special is the authors' willingness to be vulnerable and open. Each of these moving stories reminds us that we are not alone in our struggles. Each of us faces obstacles from time to time, some at times seemingly insurmountable or unbearable, to everyday difficult decisions and challenges that can make life chaotic and complicated at times. We all face obstacles, but as these authors demonstrate, it's how we respond to life situations that defines us, not what happened to us per se. So let the authors' words inspire you to find the courage and resilience to flourish in ways you never thought possible.

These stories do not promise any get-rich-quick schemes or offer any superpower solutions. I do promise, however, that the stories will touch your heart and inspire you to stay strong, knowing that you too will find the courage and determination you need to keep going. I hope you enjoy the book and are able to find some lessons and inspiration between these pages. Remember, no matter what you are going through right now, no matter how tough, confusing, or overwhelming it may seem at the time, with time, patience, and tenacity, you too can give yourself permission to flourish.

Elisa James, Th.M., M.Mus.
Speaker, Actor, Singer, Presenter, Best Selling Author
The Voice of Confidence Public Speaker Training

Chapter 1

The Strongest Mantra – KAYA MO!

Ailien Tulio

"KAYA MO!"

(You can!)

These are the 2 strong words that are always echoing in my mind. These were instilled into me by my father. These are the words that shaped me and guided me on how to live my life. These words are simple, yet they also are a profound mantra that has helped me to thrive in my daily survival, oftentimes without me knowing it.

But why am I telling you this? Why do these words or my story matter?

At the start of my writing journey for this book, I wondered why I should share my story. Why should I be part of this book that celebrates flourishing and success when I come from, what many would consider, an average family?

Growing up, I never experienced extraordinary things. We never asked for extravagant things, as we didn't know there were such things. We were content with what we had and never had the urge to ask for more.

My parents were (and still are) hard workers. They started their small business from scratch with no house, no capital, no cars or vehicles, and barely had enough to get by. We had what we needed, and we didn't feel like we were missing anything. In our own simple little minds, we were living a normal life. My parents did not show us or make us feel like we were ever struggling, but rather they displayed confidence that everything would be okay, that everything would work in our favor.

As the eldest of four children, with one brother and two sisters, I was given the responsibility of caring for my younger siblings at a young age. Growing up, I was unaware of the challenges my parents faced. Their unwavering strength and dedication to provide for our family were evident, even though their long hours at the store often kept them away from home. Despite this, my parents subtly conveyed their confidence in my ability to care for my younger siblings, instilling in me a sense of responsibility at a young age.

My parents never let us know how hard it was. They did not burden us with their worries, but rather they allowed us to enjoy our childhood and school. They showed us that as long as we kept moving forward, as long as we believed in ourselves, then we would survive and we would be okay.

I remember clearly, during my younger years, an incident when I complained that the math assignment I was given was too hard and it was impossible to solve. My father came to me, took a look at my assignment, and just said with confidence, **"KAYA MO!** There is a solution for it. It can be solved."

He did not have a college degree or diploma; heck, he didn't even finish high school, but yet, he had the confidence that I could solve it. At that moment, I remember being angry at him because he said it could be solved, but he did nothing to help me solve it. But after several hours of contemplation and trial and error, I finally cracked the problem. I still remember the feeling of satisfaction from solving it, despite the initial frustration, and something in me changed that night.

It wasn't until much later that I understood where my confidence came from. My father's response was not just a simple statement; it was more than just a personal motto—they were a philosophy of life! His words were a belief that no matter what challenges I may face, I had the power to overcome them. My parents didn't just say things; they lived what they said every day. They showed us that we will and we can survive, thrive, and flourish if we just allow ourselves to believe it was possible.

"You will and you can!"

I realize that those words are deeply ingrained in me, even when I wasn't fully aware of them. It's like a seed planted in my mind and spirit, slowly and quietly growing every day until I looked around and saw how much it has shaped me.

Even now, I am still amazed at how the incident has molded my life and how my father's words made me believe in myself. I can still picture myself and my father in that moment—where we were in the house, what shirt he was wearing, where my siblings were seated, and what my mother was doing. It is still so vivid.

Becoming a parent myself brought a new dimension to the words my father used to say. Suddenly, I found myself in my parents' shoes, faced with the responsibilities of guiding, providing, and nurturing my own children. I began to understand why they needed to believe in themselves and why they had to have that mindset. I began to comprehend the weight of my father's words in a new way. It wasn't just about my own success anymore but more so about setting an example for my kids. I realized that the best way to teach them the power of the "I can and I will" mantra is to live it every day. I started sharing my father's mantra with them, wrapping it into our daily conversations and using it as a reminder that they too have the power to shape their own destinies. If they want to be stubborn, they need to be stubborn in believing they can do it too.

When I was first approached about this book and asked to be a part of it, I was surprised and confused. *'Why me?'* I thought. In that moment, I couldn't think of anything. I didn't have a story I considered unique, moving, or inspirational enough that would matter or be worth sharing. I didn't come from wealth (but I know I was privileged). I did not have an extraordinary story filled with dramatic twists and turns like in the movies. But then it hit me—that is exactly why my story matters!

My parents did not have much; we did not have much. But what they had was a vision! They believed in themselves and in us— their children. They have instilled in us that success is not about having everything, certainly not luxurious things. Success is about making the most of what we have and constantly reminding us that we can achieve whatever we want as long as we focus and set our mind on those goals. It's about having confidence that we can achieve it even if the odds are against us.

I would like to dedicate this chapter to my parents, honoring them by sharing the lessons I have learned. It's about recognizing the power of those strong words (**KAYA MO!**- *You Can!*), how my life was shaped by it, and how the lives of my kids are shaped by them too as I impart this lesson to them. It's really about understanding that flourishing, success, and wealth are not just about material things — it's having the right mindset and confidence to reach our dreams.

As I write this, I can't help but think about my father and about how much he and my mother have accomplished. They started from nothing but had a vision, the will, and a strong determination to make it work. They had no other option but to make it work! They had faith in themselves and in each other. They did not have any roadmap, but they had each other, they had confidence and faith together.

Looking back, I came to realize that my father's words were his gift. A reminder that we all have the power to shape our destinies, no matter where we come from or what challenges come our way. They taught me that it's not about the circumstances you're born into; it's about the mindset you choose to adopt, the mindset you choose to use. It's the decision to rise above the challenge because **KAYA MO!** (You can!) You WILL achieve what you think you CAN.

As I navigate my own journey in life, I often find myself returning to those words. These words are my strength when I'm feeling overwhelmed. It's my assurance to keep moving forward even when the road is uncertain. It reminds me that I am capable of more than

I realize, that I have the power to create and shape the life I want for myself and my little family.

My chapter is my way of sharing that message with others. It's a reminder that flourishing isn't about where you start but rather where you are going and the belief that you can get there. It's all about giving yourself permission to thrive, to reach your full potential, and to live a life that is true to yourself.

In so many ways, my father's words were the foundation of what I have achieved. His words are the force that pushes me to move forward and to keep going, especially when the road is tough. They were the reason I was able to build a life for myself and my family—to create something out of nothing just as my parents did.

As I write this chapter, I hope that my story will inspire others to believe in themselves, to trust their minds and abilities, and to know that they too can achieve whatever they set their mind, soul, and heart to. Because at the end of the day, I believe that's what flourishing is all about—it's about believing that YOU WILL and knowing that YOU CAN.

So, if you are reading this and wondering if you have what it takes to succeed, then let me leave you with the same words my father left me. Hold on to them, let them be your guide, and use them as your assurance that whatever challenges you will face, you ALWAYS have the power to overcome them because you can— **"KAYA MO!"**

ABOUT THE AUTHOR

AILIEN TULIO

Ailien (pronounced as Aileen) is a dedicated mother, wife, and entrepreneur with a passion for empowering others. With 13 years of corporate experience and a seamless transition into virtual assisting, she brings invaluable insights and strategies for coaches looking to expand their online presence. Ailien's expertise spans across working with coaches from various niches, where she has developed a deep understanding of the unique challenges professionals face.

Her virtual assistant skills, particularly in social media management, are central to her ability to help businesses thrive online. She specializes in tasks such as content strategy development, audience engagement, platform management, and performance data analysis. Through this chapter, Ailien shares her personal journey and the mindset that has helped her succeed.

Contact Information

Website:	http://www.authority-branding.com/aiz
Phone number:	(+63) 976-217-508
Email:	ailientulio@gmail.com
Email Alt:	ailiengestopa@yahoo.com
Facebook:	https://www.facebook.com/udontkn0wmeyet
Instagram:	@udontkn0wmeyet

Chapter 2

The Courage to Persevere and Change

Stephanie Sullivan

A significant part of courage is making difficult decisions, like when to persist versus when to pause, take a step back, or let go and walk away. This can be particularly difficult when we feel a strong urge to persist with something. I have faced this challenge in my own life, as well as helping my clients and counselees through similar experiences. For example, realising that the career you've worked hard towards no longer suits your new life-stage, personal needs, and priorities. Or, staying in an energy-sucking workplace or relationship where you are underappreciated or nearing burn-out, but continue persevering rather than start anew. When something no longer works for us, we need to give ourselves permission to make a change and take proactive steps to execute that change. This is courage.

This has rung true for me in my personal journey. Some poignant moments include giving myself the permission and courage to relocate overseas for work (and love), prioritising my health, and orchestrating two significant career changes in my 40s. The most difficult part was discovering that something I had contributed so much of myself to was no longer my ambition, and accepting that my personal life priorities were changing.

In my early 30s, I got the opportunity to go overseas (from the USA to Australia) for work. Besides being excited to experience

Australia, I was also longing for personal space and time to focus on myself. After weeks of contemplation and sorting out logistics at home (my two cats, dog, house, and live-in sister), I said "yes," and boarded an over 24-hour long flight across the USA and the Pacific.

While I was hell-bent on being single for a while and focussing on myself for a change, about 4 weeks after arriving in Australia, I met my husband. Isn't it usually when we've made a determinate decision then the universe throws us a curveball? Well, I definitely wasn't prepared for this one.

Fast forward past six years of spending almost every weekend together, we got married. That probably seems long, but the timeline dragged out given the difficult decision about one of us relocating overseas.

Already together for six years, we were keen to try for children immediately. After a few months of trying to conceive (and that nagging feeling that the clock was ticking), we initiated testing to understand our fertility health, or any issues potentially interfering with our chances to conceive. We were pleased to learn that there were no issues. Now past the age of 35, the milestone for declining female fertility, the doctor recommended we take oral medication and supplements for a few months to help. Still without success, we were confronted with the label of "unexplained infertility" and recommended to consider IVF treatment. Only a few months later, at my age of 38, we started IVF.

I didn't expect to be struggling to conceive in my mid-30s when other women in my family were successful. At 43 years old, my mother had my youngest sister, the last of 5 children. My maternal great-grandmother also had her last of seven children at 43 years old. Given no issues had been identified, we thought IVF would be a quick solution with a given outcome; however, that was not the case.

I was going through extensive rounds of IVF, at times every other month, while also working ridiculous hours and being under extensive work-related pressure and stress. As I had been performing well over the past 15 years, I was now being considered for promotion to Partner. That carrot was being dangled over my head, keeping me jumping through hoops to meet demands and reach this achievement. I was working late nights and often weekends, then getting up at 4 AM on Monday mornings to fly interstate for work.

Managing the logistics of fertility treatment alongside any job is difficult, but regularly working interstate adds another level of complexity. The treatment starts the day after the woman's menstrual cycle starts, leaving little control over when treatment begins and the timing of subsequent medical appointments. Medication collection is urgent (same day), and injections begin the next day. I needed to self-inject different hormones at the same time every morning and night for 10–12 days. While I could be away from home for this part of the treatment, there is unpredictability and urgency in securing the medications, which are not readily available at most pharmacies. Additionally, travelling through airport security is difficult with a cocktail of supplements, needles, and vials of liquid (some chilled with an ice pack).

The second week of treatment involves multiple visits to specific pathology and radiology centres or hospitals every day or two for blood draws and ultrasounds to assess progress. You only get two days' notice for the egg retrieval surgery. Over the next several days, you wait for the good or bad news. If all goes well, 3-5 days later you return for the embryo transfer and told to rest.

For two years, I persisted because I was so close to making Partner. Most people who haven't been through this process don't understand how involved it is, so very few people were understanding at work. Despite the challenges, I managed the demands of my career and IVF so well that most of my coworkers didn't know what I was going through. I continued to perform well at work, but the ongoing stress of trying to manage a demanding career alongside fertility treatment was draining.

After many failed IVF cycles and struggling to manage my treatment and travel demands, I requested my doctor write a letter stipulating travel restrictions for medical treatment. I thought this would be taken seriously.

When I took the letter to the young HR representative, the response and counsel I received was that it would be, "Very much looked down upon if this was logged (seen) in the staffing system."

I really couldn't believe it! There were projects and clients where I lived. I was so tired of having the same conversation repeatedly with each new person (and mostly men) who wanted me to work interstate.

At this point I had enough, so I firmly replied, "Let me be clear, put it in the damned system!" And I walked out of the room. For the record, I get my boldness from my mother.

Thankfully, this helped reduce the demands for me to travel. Balancing work and fertility treatment became easier to manage. However, I was still working ridiculous hours and realising that the work stress was unhealthy and probably not helping my fertility chances.

I felt like my body was failing, incapable of carrying the load — an extremely demanding career and fertility treatment combined was too much. After "soul searching" and considering my priorities, I was less interested in the carrot over my head. My priorities were changing. More than anything, I wanted to be a mum, but to do that, my health had to come first. And once I became a mum, I wanted to be present and available, not have someone else bonding with my child while I was away for work.

But, to have that, it seemed that I would have to walk away from the career I had worked so hard at for decades, including walking away from promotion to Partner. I would have to leave behind my personal career aspiration and the expectations of others, and instead focus on my personal life priorities, desires, and wellbeing. In moments like these, we need to give ourselves permission to prioritise ourselves and permission to make a change without seeking the permission or approval from others.

At the age of 40, I decided to walk away, which was a difficult decision and transition for me. Even though the decision was based on my own priorities and needs, it still felt like grieving a significant loss because it was something I had been pouring myself into and had been consuming my life for almost two decades; however, at the same time, the decision was long overdue as I had been stressed, overworking, surviving on minimal sleep, struggling to balance it all, and feeling unhappy, unhealthy, and unfulfilled for quite some time.

I didn't fully realise how much the work pressure and stress were impacting my overall health and wellbeing until after I made the career change. I almost immediately noticed a significant difference in how I felt once I turned off the decades-long adrenaline pump from stress. I rediscovered what it felt like to have a tension-free neck, shoulders, and head.

My body was struggling to perform and cope with work demands, so how could it support the additional strain of conceiving and carrying a child successfully? Realising the physical impacts, I began researching the impacts of stress on the body, including hormones and fertility. This learning brought disappointment that through all the treatment with multiple fertility doctors and specialists, none of the doctors ever spoke to me about my lifestyle, the associated stress levels, and the impact it can have on fertility.

Thankfully, I was already taking actions to reduce my stress and improve my lifestyle and wellbeing. My new job was a dream — higher salary, with less hours, no travel, better maternity leave benefits, and more interesting and fulfilling work.

Normally, even in crazy demanding times, my energy level was high, but for some reason it was now crashing like I had never experienced before, and this continued for many weeks, maybe months. I did not understand what was going on, and I thought something was seriously wrong with my health. In retrospect,

I believe it was my body adjusting and recovering from decades of stress. After a few months, my energy returned to normal, and we started getting better fertility outcomes, including multiple pregnancies in the first year of my new career. Unfortunately, most of these ended in first trimester miscarriage.

After 14 treatment cycles, 10 egg collection surgeries, and 12 embryo transfers over 2 ½ years, at the age of 42, I was successfully carrying a pregnancy for the first time past the 12-week mark. Exactly six weeks shy of my 43rd birthday, we welcomed our miracle son into the world. Coincidentally, the embryo was transferred on my mother's birthday, and I was the same age as my mother and great-grandmother when their last child was born.

Not quite a year after our son was born, we commenced IVF again, trying for a second child. In a 12-month period, we did five IVF cycles with egg retrieval, but got only one embryo suitable for transfer, and although it was graded the highest quality, it did not result in a pregnancy. We tried again a few months later and got another embryo, which did not result in a pregnancy. Then COVID hit. Hospitals were overloaded with sick patients, and consequently at times IVF procedures were classed as "non-essential" surgical procedures and were unavailable, plus it wasn't somewhere you want to be unless you had to. We tried one more time when feasible and comfortable, but unfortunately it wasn't possible to conceive a second child despite a total of 21 treatment cycles, 16 egg collections, and more than a dozen embryo transfers. Our eight-year fertility journey was ending.

When I share my story, I often get asked two questions:

"How did you keep going and trying after so many failed attempts?" and "How did you manage the stress and emotions through all this?"

As an outcome-driven, high-achiever, I thrived on "you work hard, you get a good outcome." This experience was a big lesson that this isn't always the case. In fertility, there are so many things we don't have control over, and questions that don't have answers. When going through life's difficult challenges, there are things that we can and cannot influence or change. What helped me was learning to distinguish between the things that I could control or influence, and the things I couldn't. Then I focused my energy and attention on things that I could control or influence, and predominantly that was my own health and wellbeing. I focused primarily on having a healthy diet, stopped drinking alcohol, religiously took all the recommended supplements, did acupuncture for fertility, and reduced my stress. Although I had done my best, we still faced a lot of disappointments and upsets along the way, so I had to accept that those things were out of my control. I saw no benefit in beating myself up over something I could not control or change.

While my journey to motherhood was difficult, it has taught me so many life lessons about perseverance, wellbeing, permission to change, and relinquishing control. These have helped me not only with parenting, but also in my broader life and with coaching others. When our personal priorities, needs, or circumstances change, we need to grant ourselves permission to change, and not look to others for permission or approval. Nowhere is it written or committed that we must stay the same course or beaten path. While it takes courage to persist/persevere, often it takes more courage to change course, walk away, or relinquish control. Have the courage to put yourself first and do what is best for you.

ABOUT THE AUTHOR

STEPHANIE SULLIVAN

Stephanie Sullivan is a certified Life Coach, Health Coach, NLP Practitioner, member of the Global Coaching Association (GCA), and founder of Elevate Your Life Coaching PTY LTD.

After 25+ years in demanding, high-stress corporate roles as a business consultant, then a corporate executive, she knows first-hand about stress and trying to balance career and parenting demands, along with personal needs and wellbeing. This invaluable, real-life experience enables her to bring a realistic and pragmatic approach to coaching.

Stephanie helps business executives and professionals to boost self-confidence, courage, and personal wellbeing. She is passionate about performing her best at work and home without reaching burnout or constantly sacrificing one for the other.

Contact information can be found on the next page.

Contact Information

Website: www.elevateyourlifecoaching.com.au
Email: steph@elevateyourlifecoaching.com.au
Linked-In: https://www.linkedin.com/in/stephanie-a-sullivan/
https://www.linkedin.com/company/elevate-your-life-coaching/
Facebook: https://www.facebook.com/profile.php?id=100066764244415

Chapter 3

Facing the Existential Crisis

Melanie Naumann

"Don't live life like driving down a dead-end street."

What's courage? Is it jumping down a 40-foot waterfall? Standing up for someone who gets verbally tortured by a club of frightful chickens? Is it learning how to skateboard when you're past your prime? Is it traveling on your own to places you've never been? Walking through the dead of night? Going to the dentist? Confessing your love to someone who does not feel the same? Maybe it's quitting the 9-5 job, starting your own business, and not knowing how the money will come in. Some might consider some things foolish, while others see them as brave. So, let me ask you again: What's courage?

No matter what story I tell you, it might not even be a big deal for you. Honestly, I struggled to find a story that shows you my five seconds of bravery because it doesn't take more than a couple of heartbeats to step into the unknown, and as Nike says: *"Just do it."* Whenever something I am afraid of comes up, I ask myself: Is it worth going through it considering the possible outcome? If yes, I plunge into the ice-cold water and do it.

Still, there was one moment where my heart was beating so hard it felt like it wanted to break through my chest, crawl up my throat, and keep my tongue from saying: *"Yes, let's do it."*

There I was. Walking up and down the hospital room, dressed like the patient in My Chemical Romance's story of *The Black Parade*, waiting for the *"don't-give-a-damn pill"* that the doctor had promised me—wondering if I would survive or die.

It all started with jumping down that 40-foot waterfall in Norway. Before that jump, we eased into cliff jumping by leaping down a 16-foot cliff. I held my nose to keep the water from getting in and jumped.

Splash!

The adrenalin kicked through my veins, making me look for a bigger challenge. Another cliff, 40-feet tall, something I had never done before. The guide told us to jump into the white water of the waterfall because that's the deepest place. I ran up, jumped, held my nose, and crashed into the water. My elbow hit the surface—so hard the water felt like a wooden board, but instead of the board breaking, it was something inside my nose. It didn't bleed. It only hurt. I kept it to myself, not wanting to ruin our honeymoon. After all, as long as something doesn't seem like a problem, it's easy to ignore it. And after some time, the pain disappeared, and I forgot about it.

Years later, I found myself at an optician to pick up my new glasses. And something was off. It felt like my glasses were not in the middle of my face but slightly to the right. So I asked the optician to straighten it, who told me it was not the glasses that were askew. *(Thanks for that.)* I went home and looked at myself in the mirror, interrogating that person with the intense stare of my eyes. The only answer I got was: Yes, that bold lady was right. The tip of my nose had shifted over the years, slightly, as if it were taking sides. The worst thing was that it had become a lot harder to breathe. As an ENT physician told me, my nasal septum was so lopsided as if it wanted to be the first septum in the world to make a vertical to horizontal shift—the only option to fix this: an operation with general anesthesia.

Suddenly, I had a decision to make. And the thing about a this-or-that choice is that it marks those crossroad moments in your life where you can either decide to follow the path you're already on or dare to take a new road—which means, as Bilbo Baggins said: *"There is no knowing where you might be swept off to."*

After pushing off that decision, I finally made the appointment at the hospital and attended the medical interview. By this point, I still thought I could pull back any time and tell my husband: *"Get me the hell out of here!"* And all this time, my mind was not yet made up. It turns out that I was not scared of the surgery itself. The thing was, I did not want to give up control. I've never been unconscious, knocked out, or under anesthesia. I like to be aware of what's going on. However, a surgery like this required me to be injected with some kind of drug my body had never ever tasted (not that my body knows any drugs at all. My teenage punk heart still keeps me straight-edge).

Knowing I had to be put to sleep (who knows for how long), marked the moment of my existential crisis, which is reckoning with your physical death, your lack of real power, and your lack of control —the whole cocktail of that all at once. I paced through the room, already wearing my hospital gown, and went through my crisis. For me, doing the operation meant, if successful, I would be able to breathe better, but, worst-case scenario, I could die. They could hammer through my brain. My heart might not be able to take it. Perhaps I have an allergic reaction? Or maybe it's the day when the Zombie Apocalypse begins? Who knows? Yes, even that scenario was possible, as every storyteller understands: We *LIVE* in what-if scenarios.

My feet dragged me over the floor. I still had not decided whether to pull through with my choice, weighing the pros and cons. Calculating that risk took me from my possible death to considering what it would do to my family and the impact I hoped to make one day. Dying would mean that I would leave my kids without a mom, and I would kiss dirt before I had put a dent in the universe—the plan of *"Dream it. Do it. Leave Your Legacy"* cut short. On the other hand, I could have pulled back and doubled down on how it is. At one point, I would not have been able to breathe through my nose anymore, which can shorten one's life. In the long term, I would probably eat grass a little sooner, but in the short term, I would survive. This meant I could still play with my kids and do some sports but always be the one catching flies with my mouth. I could continue my work but run out of breath or sound like I was having a cold all year round. And I had just started singing lessons—so a snuffy sound wasn't the kind of voice I was aiming for.

I kept pacing and pacing through the room. They had promised to give me a pill to calm my nerves but had forgotten about it. Minute after minute, the time stretched, keeping me locked in that crisis. I thought about running away. No one could force me. And the more I waited, the more I asked myself why I was so scared.

The answer was simple: I had never experienced something

like this before. And that is what life is all about. After all, we constantly go through moments that are new to us. When we're a baby, everything's new. And we look fascinated at the world with wide-open eyes—seeing a world full of possibility. Once we get older, we start facing those crises that pose a REAL CHOICE between incompatible options with meaningful stakes. Lots of people stay where they are—in their comfort zone. In that place, they know what actions lead to which outcomes, and through that certainty, they feel safe—at least until something irrevocably changes. Suddenly, their whole world is upside down, and they cannot (or barely) adapt to the change because they are not used to *"cultivating change."* The truth is that change is part of life. And we have a say in it. We can influence our fate in less than 5-seconds of bravery. As I was rolled into the white-tiled surgery room, I still had the option to say 'no,' but it was the last few seconds before they put me under anesthesia that I could have pulled back.

I did not.

Embracing change means also making change happen for yourself. We have to be courageous if we want to move on and not stay stuck. Of course, we don't have certainty of the outcome of our choices. All we can do is make an outcome prediction. This means we can never be sure of the consequences of what will happen. Because we never know. And so, every meaningful decision we make that goes in the direction of where we aspire to be (despite the stakes and sacrifices) is a courageous choice, no matter in what area. Life requires us to make bold choices to have a better life and live a life worth living. If we say no to everything that crosses our path, we will never get anywhere—we will never experience the best of life.

We have to show courage on so many levels. Sometimes, we face life-and-death stakes. Sometimes, we feel like our safety is threatened, and sometimes, our relationships, status, or even who we will become. We constantly get tested. And we always have the option to be brave, "*just do it,*" and take the next step even though we don't know if we will fall or fly. A huge part of this is being okay with being vulnerable because if you dare to do something, you risk getting hurt and collecting a few scratches—in whatever way that may be, but the reward might just be worth it. I can breathe again—I survived. And collecting those scratches? It's so darn worth it.

So, let me return to the quote I mentioned in the beginning: *"Don't live life like driving down a dead-end street."*

We often see our lives and how things are as fragile. We don't want anything to change. When we can leave it as is, most people choose to keep living in that conformity of their known world, but that's choosing to live on a dead-end street because it will never go anywhere. Think of all the stories you've ever read or been told—every hero had the guts to enter an unfamiliar world. That's the place of opportunity and growth and, ultimately, transformation. It's the soil for growing into a better person who is more adaptable to changes that may come their way. So don't hold onto the image that life's got to be perfect, like a new car. You're bummed when it gets its first scratch.

Live life like you're riding a skateboard because once you get a new skateboard, you can't wait to test it out and get the first scratches on it. Riding a skateboard is about commitment. Leaning in. It's about falling and getting back up again. Skateboarders don't quit. They chase the new things—things they've never done before.

They collect the scratches on their board like scars to be proud of because every ride is worth it. As you feel every turn and all the ups and downs under your feet, it keeps you grounded and occasionally lets you fly.

So, what's courage?

It's saying "yes" to dare a little (or a lot) more. Start living. Start growing. Start pursuing your dreams because you only have one life. And if you fail, remember: it's better to fall off a skateboard and get back up and continue the ride than crash your car into a wall because then you cannot drive it anymore. It's all about the journey, and you are already on yours. And if you wonder now what your five seconds of bravery might have been, then know it's not about that one particular moment in your life. It is about looking at all the choices that led you along the path into the unknown and discovering what lies beyond.

ABOUT THE AUTHOR

MELANIE NAUMANN

Melanie Naumann is a professional song lyric developmental editor and Story Grid Certified Editor. She helps songwriters craft meaningful and compelling lyrics by harnessing the power of storytelling. She has broken down hundreds of song lyrics to find the patterns of what makes them successful – discovering why some songs fade away while others stay with us for decades or even become the anthem of an entire generation. It's her calling to help songwriters write lyrics that have the power to move the audience, keep them engaged, and let the songwriter communicate what matters to them so that it resonates deeply with their listeners, and with that: leave their legacy. When Melanie is not exploring stories, she loves to pursue her dreams: learning how to skateboard, sing, or get her black belt in Karate.

Contact Information

Email: info@lyricmastery.com
Website: www.lyricmastery.com

Chapter 4

Bonding with the Inner Child

Leyla Mesic

I was wrapped like a powerless caterpillar with all of these white cables all over my body but with a glowing tan and freshly done turquoise blue nails. It had not indeed sunk in as to what had happened. The piercing noise of the monitors was steadily echoing in my ears—was I still alive?

Then, suddenly, the sterile see-through glass door opened, and a friendly face peaked at me, sarcastically joking: "Oh, you are not brain dead? I have to talk to you; I'm not used to that."

It dawned on me that this wasn't just one of these nightmare dreams; I was indeed in the ICU of a New York hospital, and my nurse had just entered the room. I had suffered a 'Subarachnoid Hemorrhage' (SAH), which is bleeding in the space below one of the thin layers that cover the brain. It's often caused by head trauma and/or a ruptured brain aneurysm. About 10 to 14 out of 100,000 people annually experience a SAH in the United States. It's a severe condition; half of the people experience sudden death or die in the hospital, and if they even make it, they usually have a disability. Only one-third return to normal function. Why was I one of them?

I felt a pounding guilt in my chest when I took my first shower after weeks, and I couldn't comprehend if I was sobbing because

I had experienced a sheer miracle by the grace of God or because I was washing off guilt for being alive. I know I should be eternally grateful that I have been given a second chance at life, and trust me, I very much am with every fiber of my being, but witnessing people in excruciating pain, paralyzed, whimpering like a tortured dog—how could I not feel this profoundly aching grief for how much suffering there is in this world and how easy it is to look away and to forget about the voiceless and the less fortunate. I have deep humility and respect for anyone suffering and in pain and feeling hopeless or 'less than.' It is effortless and human to take life for granted, but truthfully, it could end any second, and we never know.

Let me start from the beginning of this story.

Two years ago, in the summer, I went on a vacation and allowed myself to take time off after many years of pursuing goals, not truly ever resting, honoring myself or my body, and giving my inner child freedom to play. At first, I felt guilty for just spending and not being productive. Productivity has been my go-to safety layer for so many years, and I realized how much I had measured my own worth by it. Indeed, my victimizer's voice still kicks in telling me this story, but aren't we all a work in progress, and haven't we been programmed over generations to believe that our worth directly correlates with our ability to be 'successful,' 'survival of the fittest'?

Luckily, I managed to allow myself to enjoy the time out and to move into self-love and self-care by gifting myself the art of being. The reason I am bringing this up is that, indeed, life is fragile, and if I had not enjoyed this precious time, I would have regretted it forever because the week after I returned to the city,

I ended up having a stroke. So please, my first call to action is to enjoy those precious moments gifted to you—if you can, whenever you can, go easy on yourself.

Coming home from a busy day, I was standing in my kitchen, texting a friend, when suddenly, I felt like I pinched a nerve in my neck. I wondered how that happened because I was sure I had been standing up straight. The next moment, I felt a massive 'thunderclap' headache, and my jaw was aching. My neck had become stiff, and I could barely move my head. Then, all of a sudden, everything turned black, and I thought I might lose consciousness. I realized my door was locked and I was alone. Everything happened within milliseconds: "How am I going to open that door? No one will find me if I pass out. I have to make it to my neighbors." Somehow, I focused all my energy and strength, opened that door, and knocked on my neighbor's door, who was luckily home. I also had planned to get a drink with my friend that night. When she arrived, I felt so sick.

The ER was a mess. I was standing there with no opportunity to sit while I was vomiting my brains out, and it took my friend screaming for help until someone would pay attention. They would finally take pictures of my head and send me home with the conclusion that this was a virus, which didn't feel right. I was about to get up and put on my shoes when they suddenly grabbed my bed and sent me to a room with a sign saying: "High risk!"

Then my doctor came in, shaking like a leaf, and I asked her, "What is going on? Why are you shaking like that?"

She responded, pale like a ghost, "You are having a stroke!"

I remember thinking she must be joking; everything felt so surreal—like I was in the wrong movie. My mind was utterly calm while my body was in shock and started trembling, but I also felt this deep surrender, peace, and complete faith. From that moment on, everything went fast; they gave me a bunch of medications to prevent further damage and sent me to the ICU of Neurology. I don't remember how I even got there or got into my hospital gown, but I remember talking to my dear friend, saying goodbye, and thanking her for her friendship. Honestly, I was not sure at all that I would survive this, and I knew it was a very close call.

Soon after, they had to go inside my brain to get a clearer picture of what was wrong. It is scary to do this for the first time, not knowing what they will find, how severe it is, trusting in the unknown because you are awake for the procedure, and they only put you to sleep if they find something to operate on. In the OR, I felt like a padded astronaut on a cloudy, warm moon, thinking: "I trust, I surrender, I am scared, but I am okay if this is the end for me." I experienced a level of faith that I did not know existed until that moment. I thought I had faith before, but sometimes, we don't honestly know how much faith we have until we find ourselves in a challenge.

The first time, they couldn't see clearly because there was too much blood in my brain, but luckily, they did not find anything immediate to fix. The brain is complex, but it seemed an artery had ruptured and bled into the brain. Going inside your brain doesn't hurt, but the whole procedure is uncomfortable—especially doing it several times, knowing you have to trust a person you don't know is inside your most precious computer that controls your whole body, your head taped to the surface, so you don't move anything.

The most challenging part was being home alone in the recovery phase and not truly getting the help I deserved because I didn't advocate enough for myself, and I didn't fit in. I was somewhat able to function compared to other cases. Being without family and spending a lot of that time in solitude was scary. I dealt with PTSD, and every headache or dizzy spell made me fearful of having another stroke. I was afraid to lock the door or go to sleep, worried about not waking up the next day. I had trouble doing everyday chores; I could barely walk, lift a cup, or pack a bag without crying, and I was afraid to ask for help and bother people. I am a foreigner, and living alone is hard when something like this happens. This brings me to the next point: 'Asking for help and the ability to receive it when it's available — and allowing others to take care of you, because you aren't meant to do it all alone.'

For most of my life, I have been a giver, and while it's part of my nature and I love to give — it also stems from a core wound from childhood. It's been much safer to give than receive, and it's difficult for me to take up space and have a voice but I think there are many of us. There I was in an impossible situation where I almost died, and I was still afraid to ask for help. It makes me incredibly sad, but I know life is a journey, and we are all learning, growing, being human, and trying our best.

I believe there are many layers to this life and why things happen, but on a deep level, I know this was a screaming wake-up call from my neglected inner child, who was crying to be heard and nurtured. She wanted to be held, to feel safe, and her wounds tended to.

I would sacrifice my own needs to please others and not have enough healthy boundaries, let alone knowing that it was okay to have them in the first place or what I needed them to be in many areas of my life. In other words, I had this subconscious belief that the more I gave, the harder I worked, the more I would be loved. But that isn't the real truth; it's just a belief. It's a story I learned along the way.

Self-love is a lifelong journey. Becoming your own nurturer and tending to your needs is not selfish; it's healthy and empowering. Sometimes, we think it's an act of love to over-give (and I'm not saying help isn't needed), but I think—while that might be partly true—we also enable others in their own power and ability to grow and face a challenge. The deeper we bond with our inner child and truly advocate for healthy boundaries, the safer they will feel. As humans, we all have particular wounds and unprocessed emotional pain, and those neuroceptive sensitivities were shaped by early life experiences. Unfortunately, many of us didn't have primary caregivers (co-regulators) who knew how to tend to our emotions.

This stroke held a gift of bonding with my inner child, and I am so grateful for it. It allowed me to learn ways to reparent myself and tend to those wounds and the parts of me that never received compassion. It taught me appreciation and humility for the wisdom of my body and the consciousness of being alive and what a privilege it is to be embodied in human form. I know it can be so, so hard and dark but also beautiful. It takes courage to tend to your needs and look at the pain, embracing who you are and the new version of you that might grow from all of the challenges, to plant a seed to be you, unapologetically, and share your unique gifts with the world— because whether you believe it or not, you are worthy and enough;

you have always been.

Thank you for taking the time to read my personal experience; it is only one of many human stories, but it comes from the heart.

"To honor and accept one's shadow is a profound spiritual discipline. It is whole-making and thus holy and the most important experience of a lifetime."

— *Robert A. Johnson, Owning Your Own Shadow*

It might be a bold statement, but might I dare say that if we learn how to tend to our needs and learn how to heal our inner children, compassionately listen to others and be kind without trying to fix them, being present with non-judgmental attention, and relating to our pain with kind awareness—we can make this planet earth a better place, more united. By healing ourselves, we could possibly even reprogram the pattern of believing that our needs can never be truly met. That would lead to less competition and pressure to perform and the abuse of power and Mother Earth. Would we be able to share more of our unique gifts to help each other out and build a community? I have hope, and I do have faith.

We are all in this together.

ABOUT THE AUTHOR

LEYLA MESIC

Leyla Mesic is an artist and educator originally from Switzerland. She has a deep love of music, which led her to continuously explore and learn as much as possible about the power of sound. She has studied and become certified in Musical Theater (voice, acting, dance) and different Healing Arts Modalities (Reiki, Kundalini Yoga, breath work, sound healing, and meditation). She is studying to become a Somatic Movement Therapist (processing trauma). Through her experiences in life, she realized she wanted to build a bridge between spirituality and pop music, and explored what makes pop music healing and how to utilize sound healing tools to create conscious/ restorative pop music, or "Yoga Pop." Leyla has collaborated with other commercial pop songwriters, and some of her songs can be found on Netflix, Fox TV, Amazon Studios, USA Network, etc. She strongly believes humanity can heal the world when we come into the power of our true authentic selves.

Contact information can be found on the next page.

Contact Information

Website: www.lightofleyla.com
Email: lightofleyla@gmail.com
Facebook: https://www.facebook.com/lightofleyla
Instagram: https://www.instagram.com/lightofleyla/

Chapter 5

When the Time is Right

Shaira Beth Dillena

Sometimes life doesn't look or feel beautiful at all. It's not always rainbows and butterflies. A lot of times, it's a whole dang zoo.

"He has made everything beautiful in its time."

This is a bible verse from Ecclesiastes 3:11 that was stuck in my mind during one of the most challenging periods of my college life.

I can still remember that I had just failed a major exam that day, and the weight of that failure was crushing. I knew I gave my best because I was reviewing until midnight and had my review again before the exam. Maybe that's why it's painful and crushing, because my best wasn't enough to pass. I was consumed by a mix of disappointment, fear, and frustration. I remember walking home at that time feeling so bad, so I turned to stress eating. I was eating a yema cake made by one of my churchmates; it was sweet and yummy, but I was too bitter at that time to even enjoy it. That's where I found that Bible note. It was a sticker on top of the cake. It was as if God was talking to me through that note. It calmed me down, but I was still terrified.

I was terrified of the consequences of my failure: a delay in graduation, a waste of my parents' hard-earned money from working overseas, and most of all, the fear of disappointing them.

The failure wasn't just a setback; it was a blow to my confidence and a reminder of how vulnerable I was. It made me think twice about why I was studying engineering when I wasn't even smart enough. I was overwhelmed by the thought of falling behind while my friends graduated on schedule. Then, as if things weren't already difficult, the pandemic hit. It was a tough period—we were on lockdown for a year, financially strained because even my parents couldn't send us money since they had also stopped working, and the emotional toll of seeing my peers advance while I was left struggling.

In the midst of it all, I couldn't afford to be sad or depressed. I didn't have the luxury to dwell on it. We're not rich, so I had to adapt quickly. I tried searching online since it was the only thing I could do at that time because we were not allowed to go out. From what I remember, I was just scrolling on Facebook when I saw an ad about being a tutor to foreign students. I quickly grabbed the opportunity and clicked the apply button to be able to help with bills and refocus my energy. I became an ESL (English as a Second Language) teacher while studying.

It was a rough time because the pay is not worth the hardship, nor is it enough to pay our bills. I was studying in the morning, then working at night.

With the transition to online classes, balancing work and studying became manageable, and somehow, I made it through.

I survived college. Graduating felt like an immense relief, but it also left me with a new challenge: *adulting*. The uncertainty of what came next was scary. I was so lost.

What now?

The so-called 'real world' felt like a monster I wasn't ready to face. I forgot how many times I cried because I was unsure what to do next.

I didn't know how to face my giants. It was scary to go out to the real world and find a job where I would fit in. Once again, I became a kid lost in life. So, I just stopped.

I took a few months to regroup and reassess my life, and during that time, I was so grateful for my mother's unwavering support and my church family's strong, loving presence. My mom still supported me financially even though I was already a fully grown adult, and she never questioned me why I wasn't looking for a job and just sat at home. (Thank you, Mama! I love you.)

Their encouragement and faith kept me sane and grounded, and they never let me lose sight of my faith. I think knowing that someone is backing me up and knowing that I'm not alone in this journey is what helped me go through everything. You see, we all need someone who will keep us anchored when we are at the edge of falling apart and drifting away. Having these people in my life, I just know that I have a really strong support system. I have a safety net. I am not alone.

However, I know, even with all the support, I had to make a decision for myself. I had to step up, get my ass back up, and take action for myself. For instance, becoming an ESL tutor wasn't part of my plan; it was something I did because I needed to. But now, writing this chapter and looking back, it was one of the best decisions and actions that I made. It taught me resilience and how to juggle multiple responsibilities. I think it also gave me a sense of purpose. Knowing that I have a job, that I have something to do every day.

I am feeling so proud of myself right now that I didn't just sit around and wait for things to get better. I learned to adjust, and above all, I learned that sometimes life won't happen the way you planned it to be — and that's okay. That's okay.

All this time, I kept searching for the beauty in life. I kept asking God: "Where's the beauty in coming from a broken family? Where's the beauty in failing at school and feeling left behind? Where's the beauty in financial instability that forces your parents to work overseas just to support you and your siblings? And where's the beauty in missing out on a carefree childhood because, at 12, you had to study hard and take care of your younger sister? I was just a kid myself, you know?" Seeing how other kids have their parents with them every family day, every Christmas, or other holidays felt so unfair.

I was so frustrated from asking God, "When is it my time for something beautiful?"

Those times when I felt that everything was so bad and messy, I didn't know that that was the time God was putting something in my heart. He was teaching me patience and perseverance. I wasn't able to see it because I was so busy nagging and doubting his plans. (Ohhh, God must have been so pissed!)

But I guess here's the beauty in it: Even when I couldn't see it, even when I was tired and full of doubts, even when I kept nagging God, "When is it my time?"—I never let go of my faith. I questioned God, but I never turned away because, deep down, I knew He was with me through every struggle. I was never alone.

And now, looking back, God has been so true and faithful to His promises. He was working with me and in me at that time when I thought I was alone. It's clear to me now that He was shaping and molding me through those experiences. Though the process was hard and painful, I understand now that He was the potter and I was the clay. I won't be the person that I am today without everything that I've been through. I can say that while my faith has made me strong, I also want to thank Him for giving me the right people, the right things, and the right choices at the right time. You know, faith without action is dead, so I did not just wait there in our house, sobbing and waiting for things to magically work out. It required action.

One of the lessons I learned is that you don't have to have everything figured out right away. Yes, we're getting old, but who cares?! Everyone has their own timeline; you just have to mind yours and keep moving. Sometimes you might get stuck, feel lost, or slow, but that is completely okay. You just have to keep going, may it be small steps or big changes. You must keep going.

Today, I have a job with two amazing bosses who support and value me. I'm married and building my own family. I'm happy and content. I'm blessed beyond measure.

Life is still a dang zoo. The struggle did not stop or lessen. There's always a new one every day. What happened is I started to learn things about life, and I learned how to go with it and through it. I grew up.

So now, I think, this is what beauty looks like.

It won't always look the way we expect it to. That beauty might look like a struggle right now; it might look like you are getting left behind or it might look like you are alone. You might have to go through the process of molding, of breaking or hurting, of losing or failing, but once you get through it, I promise you, it's all worth it. Pressure makes a diamond, doesn't it?

This is what I want my readers to take from my story. First, be patient, not just with the process but especially with yourself. Give yourself enough room to grow and remind yourself that life is not a race. You are being molded, and that takes time. Second, you have to keep going. You have more power over your struggles than you think. Realize that hardships are scary, but it's not something to fear. Remember this: it's okay to be scared, it's okay to pause and cry, but it's not okay to quit. Because one day, I believe that when you look back, just like what I am doing right now, you'll see that those struggles and hardships did not break you—they made you.

What I know now is that eventually, when the time is right, everything really does become beautiful.

ABOUT THE AUTHOR

SHAIRA BETH DILLENA

Shaira Beth Dillena is a soon-to-be mom. (Currently a mum of three kids; two of them have a tail.) She is also a loving wife, living her best life in the Philippines. Shaira has a Bachelor of Science in Engineering degree, and she's now found her groove as a Social Media Manager.

But before all that, Shaira was a frustrated author of love stories as a child—her plots may have been dramatic, but her passion for storytelling was real! While her childhood frustration may not have made it past her notebook, she's so excited to finally share her own story with the world. No, it's not a love story (or maybe it is), but it's packed with all the twists and turns that make life so beautifully unpredictable.

Contact Information

Phone number: +639 69567 5897 (Philippines)
Email: shairamalibiran.va@gmail.com
Facebook: www.facebook.com/shairabethsatoremalibiran/
Website: http://www.authority-branding.com/Shai
Instagram: @shabethy_

Chapter 6

Walking Away from Success

Jai Cornell

"Poverty makes you sad as well as wise."
—Bertolt Brecht

I was dirt poor, and that poverty seeped into every corner of my life, like rainwater finding its way through the smallest cracks. Even as a child, I felt the weight of it, not just in the empty cupboards or the faded clothes I wore to school, but in the heavy silence of my parents' worry. I didn't need anyone to tell me that our life was hard; I could see it, feel it, and breathe it every single day.

But amidst the struggles, there were the voices of my teachers, strong and clear, cutting through the noise of my reality. *"Study hard, get good grades, and go to college so you can get a good job,"* they would say, their eyes filled with hope. Those words were more than just advice to me—they were a lifeline. They became the mantra I repeated to myself when the nights were long, and the doubts crept in. I held onto those words with everything I had, believing that education was my ticket to a better life, a life where I wouldn't have to worry about the next meal or the rent.

So, I studied. I poured myself into my books, spending countless hours hunched over my desk, fueled by the dream of a future that was different from my past. I pushed through high school, earned my diploma, and finally found myself in the corporate world. The times then were different. No one needed a fancy college education to make it far, and even if I desired to pursue my education further, there was no means to do so. We were poor, but not poor enough for me to receive federal aid to attend college. What little savings I had were meager, almost pathetic, as I browsed around for any other option. The last thing I wanted to do was take out a loan, pushing myself from barely floating above the surface of poverty to drowning in its grasp. I had seen too many friends and family fail for one reason or another to complete their degree, then find themselves struggling harder than ever before to pay off their debts.

"I have time. I'll try again next year."

It was hard to accept these words, but it was the only choice I had—save money or risk debt. I chose the first option, reminding myself constantly that hard work always pays off; just keep going. Following my new objective, I entered the workforce hungry for a chance to prove myself and determined to save for my future. But what we plan is never always what happens.

Less than a year after graduating high school, I welcomed my first child into the world. The college life I dreamed of was shattered, replaced instead by the cries and needs of a newborn. This should have been a time of joy; I should have been excited and thrilled at the little bundle in my arms, but as I held her, I was overwhelmed with regret and sadness. I didn't hold it against her that my dream for college had to be delayed once again. What struck me to the depths of my core was the undeniable truth that I was still below the poverty line.

Even with my job, even with my savings, I knew that times would be hard. I thought I was pushing myself to be all I could until this point, but I knew I had to push even harder.

Life continued to throw obstacles on my path, deterring me time and again from getting the college education that I desperately yearned for. It wasn't easy, but I was driven to make my dream come true.

Having returned to college in January 2004, I became a full-time undergraduate student, a single mother, and a full-time worker at two jobs. For me, it was not just about getting the degree. A degree that is not used is just a piece of paper. I had to make use of it, to prove to my children that it was possible to rise from rags to riches. They would no longer see me tired, exhausted, and struggling. I told my children (and myself repeatedly): "I will be someone you look up to, someone you can take pride in."

My goal was to accomplish something unassailable: to complete my bachelor's degree before my daughter graduated from high school. And I accomplished that, but to push the bounds even further, I decided to return for my master's degree. Two years later, I began another master's degree to expand my options within the corporate world. I was tired of being passed up for promotions or work opportunities. Despite my years (sometimes decades) of experience, my education was insufficient for the positions I wanted.

Armed with the education I desperately wanted and needed, I turned my focus toward my career. It was time to escape from the clutches of poverty (and pay back the student loans, which I was against taking out, but at the time it was the only option I had to finish my degrees).

I climbed the corporate ladder with the same determination that had carried me through school. I took on every challenge, every new project, and every late night, believing that if I just worked hard enough, then success would follow.

And it did, at least by some measures.

I reached the top, becoming the senior-most manager in my role. I had the title, the office, and the responsibilities that came with leadership. But as I stood at the pinnacle of my career, I realized that the view wasn't what I had expected. Despite all the achievements, my paycheck was far from what it should have been. The irony wasn't lost on me—I had worked my way up, only to find myself trapped in a role that paid less than what some people made working minimum-wage jobs. And the hours—those were grueling. I was the first one in the office and the last one to leave. My days stretched from early morning into the dead of night, and weekends were just another opportunity to catch up on work.

There was no time for family, no time for myself, no time to breathe. The work consumed me, leaving little room for anything else. I barely saw my spouse. Our conversations became short exchanges in passing, and the weekends we once cherished together were swallowed by the demands of my job. My life had become a never-ending cycle of emails, meetings, and reports. I was always connected, always on call, always working. The dream of success that had driven me was now suffocating me, and for all my hard work, I felt like

I was making nothing—both in terms of salary and in terms of life.

Then came the day when everything changed—the day when my morals and ethics were tested. A decision was put before me, one that would compromise everything I believed in. It wasn't a big thing, not on the surface, but it was enough. Enough to make me pause and reflect. Enough to make me realize that no amount of success was worth sacrificing my integrity. That moment was a wake-up call. I could no longer ignore the gnawing feeling that I was not where I was meant to be. I had to find the courage to change, to step away from a path that was taking me further from who I truly was.

I remember the day I decided to walk away. It was as if a weight had been lifted off my shoulders, a burden I didn't even realize I was carrying. I had no regrets as I left my corporate role in leadership. I chose to take a step back, to become an individual contributor while still being a leader in my own right. The title didn't matter to me anymore. What mattered was my peace of mind, my happiness, and my values.

For the first time in a long while, I started to reconnect with myself, with my life, and with the people who mattered to me. I made time for my spouse, for my family, and for the simple joys that I had neglected. I found joy in the things that truly mattered—walking in nature, laughing over dinner, enjoying the quiet moments that life had to offer. I learned to appreciate the balance between work and life, to embrace the present, and to find fulfillment beyond a paycheck.

It's embarrassing it took me so long to realize these lessons. Most of my life I had been running from poverty, always searching one way or another for a means to escape, to climb out of the filth that was associated with my idea of destitution. I understand now what a fool I had been—so much time, energy, and sanity wasted on chasing after an illusion of what I thought amounted to success. Money comes and goes, careers rise and fall—I will never get back the time I lost with my family. However, I'm glad that I was able to realize my mistakes. It's not too late for me.

Looking back, I realize that God knew what I needed even before I did. When I walked away, I walked towards something far more valuable than a high-paying job or a prestigious title. I walked towards a life that was true to who I was, a life where my values guided my choices. It took courage to embrace change, to step away from the familiar and into the unknown. But in doing so, I found my way back to myself, to a life filled with purpose, integrity, and joy. And I learned that is the true measure of success.

ABOUT THE AUTHOR

JAI CORNELL

Jai Cornell is a coach, speaker, and author who provides others with a platform to share their stories through the "Permission to Flourish" anthology series. Focusing on leadership development, Jai has inspired professionals in a range of industries, including aerospace. Beyond her professional work, Jai is committed to philanthropy and community service, using her expertise to promote positive change and a culture of support and empowerment. Her work as an author and entrepreneur demonstrates her dedication to creating accessible opportunities for brand growth. Jai encourages others to lead meaningful, enthusiastic lives and to pursue prosperity with self-assurance. Her passion for personal development and empowerment shines through in all she does. She hopes to inspire others to do the same—to prove that anyone can succeed with hard work and dedication.

Contact Information

Email: info@jdmwow.com
Facebook: https://www.facebook.com/yiayiacornell
Website: www.permissiontoflourish.net
Website: www.jdmwow.com

Chapter 7

Following Your Heart

Leska Prokopets

Transitions in life can be challenging to navigate through for the average adult. Imagine what it is like for a teenager. During transitional periods, we question our identity, values, and beliefs, trying to make sense of what is happening to better handle relationships, work, health, and finances to support our primary goals and objectives. More often than not, we look at these transitional periods as a threat and inconvenience to our perfectly designed life. But what if having this outlook actually robs us of an opportunity to gain insights about ourselves and the world so that we could create a new and more fulfilling life destined for us? What if life has given you an opportunity to discover and reinvent your life and raise it to higher standards? And what if the hardships are a wake-up call to learn and become authentically you as you follow your heart?

This is my story as a girl who became orphaned as a teenager and had lived a life where everything was stacked against her with no chance of surviving in the world. Everything I knew and all that was familiar was taken away at a young age to serve a higher purpose, where my life is now lived with greater appreciation and openness of heart. Since youth, life has challenged me in ways only a few people could ever understand or know. But, perhaps, you will find pieces of the story that resonate with you to bring you inspiration and hope;

to understand that challenges are here to shape us into beautiful vessels of love so that we can become bright, shining lights to the world. I hope you find solace in knowing that while you may feel lonely, you are not alone. So, let us dive deep into the story to explain what I mean.

As a teenager, I lost both of my parents and younger sibling in a car collision in Ukraine. The fact that I survived the car accident was a miracle in itself, and surgeons' prognosis gave little hope for recovery or ability to walk again. They told me I was destined to be a cripple for the rest of my life. Half of my body was structurally damaged with blood filling major organs and systems, thus shutting down the oxygen supply to the brain. Indeed, it was a lost cause scenario, yet I survived. But surviving was only half the battle. The other part was the recovery.

Would I recover? And in what condition would I be? Would I be in a vegetative state for the rest of my life? No one knew. It was a scary thought to consider that I survived only to remain a coma vigil—a helpless being whose mere existence is half awake and half asleep. But, to some extent, we are all walking half awake and half asleep, so perhaps my condition would not be so bad. That way I would be like everyone else, with nothing to offer and nothing to hide. But that did not give me solace. It did not matter that I would look like everyone else. It mattered that there was no one to relate to and nowhere to belong. I felt alone.

Now that I lost both of my parents and a younger brother, I lost my anchor to who I was. I did not know how to navigate the world as a teenager, so I learned to navigate it as an adult.

The innocence and play of childhood were no more. Surviving was the name of the game. With no one coming to protect or help me, I was on my own. But not exactly. Something within me gave me hope. I called it Beatitude—the blessed spirit—who helped me navigate the world. At this point, my older brother became my legal guardian, bringing me to the United States for the first time. I was excited to embark on the new adventure of living in a new uncharted territory with my older brother, who was my hero.

I was promised to receive medical and therapeutic care to facilitate recovery. I was promised support in transitioning to a new culture and language I did not know. Everything seemed possible with bright hope for the future until we landed in a U.S. territory and it became known that I would receive neither medical nor therapeutic care. By the time I moved to the United States, I worked my way to a wheelchair and, according to their standards, I appeared functional, which is why they withdrew their support. It felt as if I was being punished for getting better. But I brushed it off and decided to do it on my own. I figured that I am not going to let people in white coats, who claim to have medical authority, be an authority over my life.

Over time, I built confidence and courage to retrain my body and brain to full health. But I felt vulnerable and exposed—both physically and mentally. *"What if I get it wrong? What if I cause more damage?"* These were lingering thoughts in my mind. But Beatitude's voice encouraged me to keep going no matter what other people said or thought. So, I listened and followed my heart; even when doubts and fears crept in, I developed techniques to control the mind by replacing them with more empowered thoughts. They became useful in helping me navigate through other challenges that came along. Fears and doubts became my daily companions, robbing me of the joy of being alive and fully present in this world. But I would not allow them to control my life. I would not allow them to take over the life that I have been given. There was too much to get done and too much to discover. So, I let my faith be greater than my fears. That is how I lived—a walk of faith—one step at a time.

I was quickly enrolled in an English-speaking school (a language I barely knew). There was no time for respite. It was time to face reality and move forward. There was no time to grieve or heal. There was no time to heal the wounds of the broken body, and no time to heal my bleeding heart.

Every night I cried myself to sleep, weeping for answers that no one, not even Beatitude, would give. I could not understand why such a heavy burden of different responsibilities at school and life were placed on me. I could not understand why I was all alone in this journey with no one to guide me. Sure, Beatitude was with me, but most of the time it would be silent and would appear only in the most desperate of situations. I was growing bitter and angry that the world was against me and trying to eradicate my existence. I had to fight for my own existence. The world seemed to cave in, swallowing me alive. So, I had to become strong to better navigate my life. It was up to me to decide when to wake me up in the morning and go to sleep, it was up to me to complete schoolwork on time, it was up to me to work side jobs to make money and to handle money responsibly. These taught me life skills and how to work hard for the things I cared about. I raised my standards and decided who I wanted to be—that no matter what life throws at me, I will be kind. I applied myself diligently to everything in life and I became successful.

Success is a two-edged sword. On the one hand, it brings exhilaration; and on the other, grief. It's exhilarating because it unveils power, strength, and confidence within us. It also brings grief, making us unrelatable and different, which fosters envy, jealousy, and suspicion that act as enemies for true connection. We must decide which choice to make and live with the consequences of that choice. This is a path of authenticity and dignity that builds resilience, courage, inner strength, and humility.

In high school, I gained academic knowledge and theories. Outside of school, I studied nutrition, fitness, and diets based on current trends in the world. I applied them to my daily routine to improve cognition and physical performance. I trained hard, studied hard, and came out the other side surprised that the effort had paid off when I graduated high school with honors and awards. It came as a surprise because I beat the odds of me ever succeeding or even surviving in the world. It did not make sense how a foreigner who was destined for failure actually made progress. My mind could not comprehend how my health and fitness improved. It bewildered me how it became possible to learn two foreign languages in an already intensive academic curriculum. It challenged the norms, views, and beliefs I observed in the world. So, it became my life's mission to discover the intelligence of the human body and mind and how to actualize its potential. I began to discover the purpose and meaning that challenges have in shaping our lives. My heart was filled with gratitude for the guidance to embrace my authenticity as a holistic path for healing of body, heart, and mind.

I began to live a purpose-driven life, spending almost two decades studying and applying principles of wellness for peak performance. My determination and commitment to discovering life's principles and designing my life around those goals became my guiding stars as I created structures and procedures to improve life.

College was a new environment that presented new challenges. Academic demands and peer pressure grew stronger each day. There was no relief—only hustle. So, I created new routines and systems to better manage my energy and time. In college, I learned the theories and principles of neuroscience, psychology, and human physiology —brain and body health. Outside of the classroom, I worked in academic, clinical, fitness, and domestic environments to gain real-world experience to identify the efficacy of those techniques.

By implementing certain tools and techniques into my own life, I noticed patterns and correlations between time and effort, and how certain activities can be performed with greater ease. Being resourceful and efficient allowed me to produce more with less effort. Imagine getting a dopamine rush when you do something exciting! This was it for me! Each time I discovered, innovated, and created something new, it gave me a thrilling dopamine high. I discovered ways that improved health and physical performance. And, once again, I was bewildered at the possibility of grading above a 4.0 GPA, even in college.

Real-world experience opened up opportunities to gain better communication skills, learn empathy, and influence. This is the point where I realized the significance of a community. Community improves our overall well-being, boosting confidence, self-esteem, and strength. Through my contributions to the community, my heart continued to soften.

I spent almost two decades working with adults and children who taught me the real value of vulnerability, authenticity, and freedom. In my younger years, I felt I needed to be strong and guarded, but taking the role as a complementary parent took those barriers away. They deepened my understanding of influence and leadership skills in a compassionate way. And they also reawakened my playfulness once again. I was no longer half awake and half asleep. I became alive! I became vulnerable again in a way that actually fostered a connection and deep love for each individual and the planet. Perhaps, life's challenges shake things up to bring us closer instead of apart. Perhaps, life is not what it seems and calls us to step into uncharted territory of higher standards to be better leaders, parents, and friends.

Ultimately, I learned that even in the harshest storms, where everything fades away and there is no hope for the future, we can trust the way of a blessed heart. It knows the way to build resilience and strength as much as vulnerability and courage. Despite the challenges and limitations, we are made to thrive and to live by the design of our hopes, dreams, and aspirations. What if transitions were an opportunity to discover and follow your heart?

ABOUT THE AUTHOR

LESKA PROKOPETS

Growing up in the beautiful country of Ukraine, Leska appreciated the simplicity and beauty of life. At a young age, she moved to the United States, where she developed her passion for art, knowledge, and the science of the body and mind. After working in fitness, therapeutic, and professional environments, she discovered her gifts of empowerment and coaching that led her to become certified in one of the world-class personal and professional development certifications called Elite Mentorship Forum and a Leading Global Mentorship Program for business development and growth. She helps CEOs and leaders develop a resilient mindset and integrate mindfulness strategies for better leadership and business growth. She helps people reduce burnout, improve decision-making, and increase productivity for work and personal fulfillment. By bridging Eastern and Western wisdom into transformative step-by-step processes, Leska helps high-achieving CEOs and executives become resilient and adaptive while maximizing resources for strategic growth and impact.

Contact information can be found on the next page.

Contact Information

Website: www.leskaprokopets.com (under construction)
Linked-In: linkedin.com/in/leska-prokopets-92530592
Facebook: https://www.facebook.com/leska.prokopets
Appointment: https://calendly.com/leskaprokopets/discoverycall

Chapter 8

The Wave of life

Aimee Kaopua-Hersey

Growing up in Hawaii in the 1980s, I always imagined myself as an old spinster cat lady, living at home with my mom. My self-esteem and sense of worth was very low in my teens. Being bullied in middle school by my peers did not help. Yet, not once in my wildest dreams did I ever think I'd get married, have a child, and move to the mainland (aka the continental U.S.).

We moved in November 2005. It was hard to be so far away from my immediate and extended family. All I had was my husband and young son. I was moving to an unfamiliar place with no home or job lined up. We had to rely on my in-laws (God rest their souls) for everything. They helped us put a deposit down and move to an apartment near their home. My father-in-law also co-signed for my car because he had excellent credit while mine was nonexistent. My mother-in-law then helped me set up a local bank account and told me about a place down the road from their house that was hiring, which is where I applied.

The open job position was for a DSP (direct support person). I had no idea what I was getting myself into when I applied for the job. When I was hired, I found out quickly how different it was from the work I was used to. Most of my life had been spent in the food service industry, which is where I pursued my formal education and built my knowledge for a future career. I had no experience caring for individuals with developmental disabilities. It was challenging at first but became very rewarding the longer I stayed.

This December (in 2024) will mark 19 years that I've been with this inspirational organization. In that time, I've transferred and been promoted from: a DSP, cook, dietary aide, and now, a dietary supervisor. Most people originally apply because they need the money, but there are those like me that stay because it becomes a home away from home. I also love the company's mission statement: "Everyone has the right to be treated with respect, to participate in community life, to develop and exercise personal competence, to have family and friends, and to make decisions in their lives."

Before I was hired as a DSP in Dec 2005, my husband and I struggled to provide for our son. We were once reliant on WIC, which is a government program that provides funding for women, infants, and children who have little to no income. The program allows women to purchase healthy foods for themselves and necessities for their children that they otherwise would not be able to afford. I remember having to eat hot dogs with bread but being thankful that we had food to eat. There were times when I've had to check my bank balance before going grocery shopping. Trips to fast food places were a treat and not an everyday occurrence. A sit-down restaurant was by invitation only, and that was usually because the other people were paying. Going to the gas station for something other than gas, like a soda and candy, was out of our budget. I thought we were "big ballin" when we transitioned from the Dollar Tree to Walmart, then from Walmart to Meijer. Until you've had to go from name brand to store brand food because you can't afford the higher price— don't judge.

Like the Bible verse Matthew 7:1 says, *"Judge not lest ye be judged."*

Reflecting back on all the hard times during my move to Illinois, I see now how far I've come in life and wouldn't trade it for anyone else's life experiences. It's helped make me into the person I am today. Being raised by a single mother, 3 older siblings, and also by my maternal grandparents—I knew I was loved. Going to church every Sunday morning was non-negotiable, but I learned to love it. I miss the Tuesday night Bible study gatherings we used to have at the homes of different family members. We'd eat dinner, sing hymns, quote Bible verses in Hawaiian, and learn about God's word. There'd be outer island visits to sister churches for week-long summer retreats as a youth, which progressed to adult leader as the years went on. I'm pretty sure that's where my potential for leadership got started (besides becoming an aunt at the young age of 11).

Being blessed as an aunt at such a young age with so many nieces and nephews, I was able to share in some of their care and raising. (Of the 19 nieces and nephews I currently have, I helped to raise the first 8.) I helped my sister-in-law as an assistant soccer coach with my nephew's then-5-year-old team. That was fun! I remember playing "taxi" to my eldest sister's kids while they were in elementary. I'd either take them to my mom or grandma's house (where I was staying at the time). We'd have a snack, get homework done, play awhile, and wait for my sister to pick them up after work. There were times at the annual weeklong summer fun church events where, because I was 18 and technically an adult in the eyes of the law, was gifted the role of adult leader. We went to many different locations on the island that was hosting for that year. Each adult leader was entrusted with the care of at least 15 children and had 2 junior leaders as helpers. The many children I supervised in those programs will always have a special place in my heart, especially the rascal ones. I can only hope they hold me in the same regard.

    The first of two pivotal moments in my life where leadership was given to me was by my family. When my mother became extremely ill during the COVID pandemic in January 2022, I flew home to Hawaii from Illinois for a week. If not for my mother-in-law's passing in December 2021, from which the sale of her jewelry funded my airfare home, I would not have been able to afford that trip. (I kept reminding myself: Trust in God; He always provides.)

    When I arrived, my siblings and I had a sit-down meeting about our expectations with each other and the continued care that our mother would need. As the youngest of four, I never expected to be the one leading the discussion. I always deferred to my older siblings for guidance, but this time it was different. With my background in not only food service but also healthcare, I was the one being looked to for guidance. I made a list of things to go over with them, and it went better than anticipated. Thankfully, my mom is still with us and will continue to be here with us for years to come.

    The second pivotal moment in my life where leadership was thrust upon me was when the former dietary supervisor retired. Though her position was given to someone else (and the person they hired did not return to work after contracting COVID), the food service director asked me if I could help out for the time being. Eventually, I was asked if I wanted the position. I knew I could do most of what the job entails, though at the time I did not know all that it encompassed.

I just did not think I was deserving, worthy, or confident enough to be in charge. This was my dream job after all: 40-hour work week, Monday through Friday, no weekends or holidays unless someone called in sick, plus a bigger pay raise. So, I did what my mom used to do when she needed an answer but was unsure. I prayed about it and asked God for guidance. Then I opened my Bible and read the two words I was looking for: "Go forth."

In April 2022, I accepted the position and was transferred.

Though I've had a lot of ups and downs professionally, mentally, physically, and emotionally, I didn't let it hinder me spiritually. My faith has always been that one constant in my life. It's what has brought me through "the waves of life," as I like to call them. It hasn't always been a smooth ride. There's definitely been a time or two where I felt like I was drowning or treading water instead of riding the waves. One of the worst moments I found myself drowning was when my husband had to have brain surgery for a pituitary adenoma back in October 2023. He pulled through and is doing well, but there were months of recovery. During those months, I provided care while also working as a full-time dietary supervisor and balancing my own health issues, which requires meticulous monitoring, medication, and diet. But I give all the glory to God because I know that if He brings me to it, He's going to bring me through it.

To you, dear reader, I leave you three important lessons.

My first lesson to you comes from the hardship I faced when I first moved from Hawaii to Illinois, which is that you can't always expect the same in others that you do for them. When you give, you give because you can, not because of what you'll get in return. Yet, in the same breath, don't let them take advantage of you or mistake your kindness for weakness. I've gotten help from so many people, but I've also been used so many times by different people with different circumstances.

My second lesson comes from a colleague I worked with: "Just do your job; don't let the job do you!" I'd get frustrated with an employee for calling in sick at the last minute knowing I'd have to go in if no one else was available to work. There were also times when I was called at home, off the clock, about an issue with menu items not being found and having to substitute with another day's meal. I always attributed myself to being a very thoughtful and giving person, trying to "live aloha." Or, in simpler terms, treat others the way you would want to be treated. However, I've also learned to set boundaries and stick with them. Work needed to stay at work, and my off time belonged to me.

My final lesson to share comes from my faith: *"Trust in the Lord with all thine heart and lean not unto thine own understanding. In all thy ways acknowledge Him and He shall direct thy path"* (Proverbs 3:5-6). These Bible verses help me live day-to-day. Trusting that there is always hope for every situation; therefore, there is always joy to be had. When something troublesome or difficult comes up, I seek and use patience to find a solution. And in prayer, I have faith in God, that He will provide when hope and patience have run their course.

I'm still alive, and life didn't break me like I thought it would. Don't let the low moments in your life get you down. Live, learn, and keep riding the wave of life.

ABOUT THE AUTHOR

AIMEE KAOPUA-HERSEY

Aimee Kaopua-Hersey currently works as a dietary supervisor for a private, not-for-profit organization that provides round-the-clock care for individuals with developmental disabilities in Rockford, Illinois. She was born and raised on the island of Oahu, where she earned her Associate's of Applied Science degree in food service. She has excelled beyond her humble origins, earning awards and accolades within the culinary industry. Her desire to be the best that she can be, along with hard work and dedication, has earned her one of the highest positions within her organization's department. Aimee's hobbies are centered around cuisine, which she finds joy in sharing with others. Her ambition is to maintain a happy medium in this journey called Life by always moving forward and never giving up—a lesson that she wishes to pass on to the readers through her chapter.

Chapter 9

Flip the Script

Issabele Popescu

*"Change the way you look at things,
and the things you look at change."*
— *Wayne Dyer*

It was a beautiful sunny Sunday morning, I was excited about all the things we would do with our kids as I prepared breakfast for them. I still remember that morning. I made pancakes and began to fill them with some plum jam that I had prepared a week ago. You could smell the vanilla pancakes' sweet scent all over the house. My mouth was watering, waiting for the first hot pancake to be done. I finished cooking the first one, and as usual, the first one was for me. I filled it in with some homemade plum jam, then I closed my eyes and took the first bite. It was marvellous – the perfect taste.

Even now, just remembering it, I can feel my mouth salivating.

Memories from my childhood started to appear one by one. The days when I would cook pancakes, and I would fill them in with my mum's plum jams she used to prepare every single autumn. In that moment, I was thinking that I have to call my parents.

My kids came into the kitchen one by one, attracted by the smell of cooked pancakes, and each waited for their pancake to be cooked.

Pancakes were the family dessert, and everyone loved them.

As soon as I finished, I called my parents in Romania. My father had been sick for years, and for the last few months he hadn't felt that well. I asked him how he was doing. He told me that he was okay, but that he wanted to ask me to forgive him if he was not a good father. In that moment, I knew that I needed to fly to Romania to see him one last time. I could feel it. I bought the ticket for the following day, and on Tuesday, after a 20-hour flight, I was in Romania.

He died that week on Friday night. I wanted to tell him so many things. Seeing him there, on the deathbed, breathing heavily with his eyes closed, I felt so helpless. My mum was there, crying, unable to control herself. My sister and my brother were there crying too, not knowing what to do. I could not cry; I was not ready to accept he was dying. I went close to his ear, not knowing if he heard me or not, and I told him that even if he wasn't the perfect father, he was as good as he could be, and I thanked him and told him I loved him very much. I wanted to do more, to help him somehow, to save him. I knew nothing could be done. He died peacefully. Being there, seeing him dying, changed my life in a way I could not imagine would be possible.

On the 10th of March 2019, the night after my father's passing, I realised something that, for a long time, was just nonexistent in my mind. I realised that the only certainty that I have in my life is death. One day, sooner or later, I will die, and everything will be gone.

On my way home to Melbourne, while I was flying, I started thinking about my life. I was depressed for the last 6 years, taking depression pills, overweight (almost 100 kilos), and my marriage was going down the drain since we were fighting all the time. I was smoking like a chimney. I was drinking quite a lot. The barbershop that I started 2 years before was $50,000 in debt.

I started crying, and for hours, I could not stop it. I wondered: What did I do with my life? Where had all my dreams gone?

Australia was my dream country since I was a child. Owning a barbershop had been my dream since I was 17 years old. Here I was, in Australia, my dream country, owning the barbershop that I had always desired. I also had 4 wonderful, amazing kids. My life was perfect but I felt nothing worked the way I desired it to. I felt that everything was against me, that I didn't have anyone to help me. I thought I wasn't good enough, that I wasn't worthy. I thought I was not good as a mum and that my kids were disappointed in me. I thought I was not good as a wife and that was the reason my marriage was not working. I thought my business wasn't working out because I was not good at it—not good at anything. I was the perfect victim in my mind. The more I thought about everything, the more unhappy I became. I was watching myself in the mirror, and the only thing I could see was the image of a failure.

As I said, I had the perfect victim mentality, I was telling myself more and more BS stories. And I was waiting to be saved by someone else, waiting for outside help, imagining that it would be someone else's duty to save me.

I knew that if I continued the same way, I would have the same result: depression, overweight, further loss in my business, smoking even more, and eventually drinking more in the hope that I would become numb. The truth is, I always knew that I would still wake up the following day with the same shit in my life, and this was my salvation.

So, I had to make a decision: How do I want my life to be? What path do I choose? The one that was known and would give me the same results? Or the unknown path—the one I did not know anything about and had no idea where it would take me?

Let me tell you what made me choose the right one for me.

One day, I was watching Netflix, and a documentary appeared on my screen. The name of the documentary was *I Am Not Your Guru*. It was about Tony Robbins seminar, "Date with Destiny." I decided to watch, and I was impressed by it. However, it was hard to believe that change could occur so quickly, so I did a bit of research. I started listening and watching his YouTube videos. I did this for a few weeks. I became curious, more and more curious. I wanted to know if Tony Robbin would come to Australia, and if so, when. And guess what? He was going to be here in May of that year!

I borrowed money from my husband's credit card to buy a ticket for the "Date with Destiny" event as well as flights and other accommodations. The whole thing cost me around $9,000.

I lived in Melbourne, and I had to fly to Cairns and be there for one week. Imagine this: I had to close the barbershop (which was already closed twice in the last 6 months, each time for 3 weeks), and leave my family and 4 kids behind. It was the first time, since I had been married, that I did something by myself and for myself. It was the first time when I was thinking about *me* first. And I felt so guilty and selfish: to be at the hotel by myself and to be a part of something by myself. I was so very scared.

And all this time, something inside kept telling me: "Do not believe that this event will do anything for you! It's going to be just money you lose! Go back home!"

And I was fighting with it, and I said to myself, "I want to try it anyway."

So, there I was in Cairns, ready for the big 7 days and 6 nights! And indeed, they were very big!

On the first day, I don't know how it happened, but I ended up being in the diamond area, not even having an idea about what it was. My ticket was for the gold area. I saw everyone happily chatting with each other, moving around, and waiting excitedly for Tony Robbins to come out. I felt nothing like that. I wanted the first day to finish, to prove to myself that I was right, that none of this could help me. I wanted to go home.

And then, the moment everyone was waiting for came.

Loud music played. People were dancing, jumping, and screaming like crazy as they waited for Tony Robbins to appear! I truly believed that everyone in there was crazy, and I was the only one sane. I could not understand how they could be so happy, not when I felt so miserable!

My seat was near the end of the row. I had the privilege to see and hear Tony Robbins very closely. He was a huge man with a thundering voice that made you feel unstoppable.

I was crying the whole first day. I could not dance, jump, or enjoy the moment because I was too wrapped up in my own mind. I felt it was inappropriate of me to dance or chat with anyone else. I felt so insignificant among all these happy people that I did not dare say a word for the entire day. I just listened, doing my best to understand everything.

That night I went to the hotel, and I could barely sleep. I was thinking and thinking. I analysed my whole life.

The second day was a big day. I understood that I was living the story I was telling myself, that my mind was my toxic best friend, and I was following the suggestions it gave me all the time. It was the first time I heard about the conscious mind and unconscious mind. I learned that the mind does not distinguish between something that is real and something that is not real—it takes as real whatever I put into my mind.

I learned that everything that I do in my life is linked to the way I was taught between ages 0-7. If any of the 4 personal human needs (certainty, uncertainty, love and connection, and significance) that were supposed to be filled by my parents were missing, then I was going to search to fulfill that need all my life.

I learned that the stories that I tell myself every single moment will shape my present and my future.

I learned that my weight was not due to someone making me eat more, that my barbershop was failing due to external reasons, and that smoking was my own choice.

Most importantly, I learned that it takes one second to decide what I want and how I want my life to be, and that everything starts with me.

On that same day, the day that opened my mind to a new world, the world of endless possibilities, was the day I decided my future. It was a day that I will remember all my life because that was the day I decided to change the way I looked at things, and the things I looked at changed too. It was such a hard decision to make.

Even if I was so frightened. Even if I kept wondering: "What if it's going to be even worse? What if I am going to be even unhappier than before? What if my barbershop loses even more? What if …?" So many what-ifs. Even if all of these were running through my head, in one second I decided to choose **The Unknown Changing Path.**

How I did it and the steps that I took is a story for another time.

In 1 year, my business was booming! I was making six figures. I lost 20 kilos of fat and changed my eating patterns for the better. I stopped taking depression medication because my depression was gone. I stopped smoking and drinking. I started studying everything that Tony Robbins was doing— NLP and Hypnosis, and I added in Timeline Therapy.

In 2 years, I became an internationally recognised Master Practitioner in NLP, Hypnosis, Timeline Therapy, and Coaching and started training businesses like mine.

In 3 years, I became an NLP and Hypnosis trainer, ready to support businesses and people in need.

What do I wish for the future? To support as many business owners that want to succeed in their business and life through NLP and Hypnosis and to *Flip the Script,* because, as Jim Rohn said, "Your life does not get better by chance, it gets better by change."

And always remember:

Master your mind, master your life.

ABOUT THE AUTHOR

ISSABELE POPESCU

Issabele Popescu immigrated to Australia in 2008 from Romania with her husband and two children. Over the next five years, she welcomed two more children while transforming her career and life. Issabele is an internationally recognized NLP Trainer, Hypnosis Instructor, Master Timeline Therapy Practitioner, and Master Coach. She holds double degrees in Accounting and Business Management and worked as a Chief Accountant in government institutions before deciding to change countries, careers, and her life's direction.

As the founder of **Be The Man Barbershop**, a multi-six-figure business, and **Issabele Popescu Coaching**, she empowers small business owners to transform their lives and businesses through mindset mastery. Having overcome dark times herself, Issabele is passionate about helping others do the same. She loves spending quality time with her children, swimming, and pursuing continuous personal development. Her ambition is to inspire as many business owners as possible to achieve the success they deserve.

Chapter 10

Embracing Change & Adversity for a Better Life

Chantelle Lynch

> *"You and only you are responsible for your life choices and decisions."*
> — *Robert T. Kiyosaki*

"Something has to change…" These were the words that ran through my mind as I sat at my desk, head in my hands. This was back in 2016 at my then-job, working in the public health sector. I worked inside a large, air-conditioned building on the 4th floor with windows that didn't open. Every day, I rushed into the office after dropping my 3-year-old son off at the childminder, and then battling the daily commute on the trains. Becoming a single mum and working full-time became difficult financially as well as emotionally.

Paying the rent, the bills, and the childminder—I did not have enough to cover everything, even with the help of government benefit assistance. Even when I was able to leave work on time, I was still late to pick up my son from the childminder due to trains being cancelled or delayed, incurring additional fees by the childminder.

During this time, I was also going through divorce and childcare arrangement court proceedings. The father of my son and I strongly disagreed on how best our son should be looked after, to the point that it ended up in court. The relationship with my then-husband was toxic and abusive. My self-esteem, confidence, and competence to be a good mother became weaker. Emotionally, this was one of the darkest times of my life. Our son, who was my angel, saved my life and saved me from this destructive marriage. My beautiful, special child, who had made life worth living, was going to be put in a childcare arrangement that was not going to be decided by his father or me, but the courts. Ultimately, we both had little say on what the court's decision would be, and this was terrifying.

Life felt like it was completely out of control. Everything was happening to me. I wanted freedom and flexibility; I wanted more time with my son instead of just an hour in the mornings before the childminder and evenings after work. I needed more money; I needed CHANGE.

One day, during the midst of all this, whilst at work, these words came to me completely out of the blue: "Become self-employed. Start a cleaning business."

I thought, "Eh? That's a bit odd..." But I continued to ponder the thought. "Could I really do that? Would it help? Would it work?"

To quit my job, after working within the organisation for 8 years to start a cleaning business with no experience was a huge risk. I was also studying towards my Psychology degree part-time. It was a lot to take on.

However, I did my research on how to start a cleaning business. I checked how much income I could make and if I could have flexibility around my son and school. After weighing everything up,

I decided to go for it. I handed in my notice to my employer. I was now on a ticking clock to make this work.

Change was happening.

Fast forward to the end of August 2016, 2 months after handing in my notice at my job, I was a fully booked cleaning business owner, receiving consistent 5-star reviews from clients. Everything had started to change for the better. I had more control over my life. I had more income; I could pay my bills and still have money left over. I had more time with my son, flexibility to work and study when I needed to, and around the needs of my child. I was officially an entrepreneur, making money from my own creation. This was a powerful and happy time. During this transformative time, I met and followed other business owners, entrepreneurs, and coaches, which led me to more contacts and opportunities. I decided to seize each opportunity that could help me grow and develop further as an individual, as a business owner, as well as a mother. I worked with other businesses, and became a coach within home utilities, travel, and health, wellness & beauty.

One thing I realised, as I embarked on my entrepreneurial journey to a better, more fulfilled life, was that personal and self-development were key. To really live life on your terms, which was my desire, you have to develop a strong, resilient, and focused mindset, which I did. People are not always going to agree with your decisions, support you, or embrace your desire for change. They may actively even try to stop you. If I had allowed this to happen, I can assure you that I would not be here writing this chapter for you today. Not only this, running a business, especially multiple businesses, takes dedication, time, and effort. You have to be disciplined, consistent, motivated, and have an element of skill. You have to be willing to embrace change and adapt as the times and world changes.

Part of my evolution into a better me, involved improving my health. During my time with the health, wellness, and beauty business, I became a healthier person. I wanted to be the best that I could for me, my son, and my businesses. I decided to eat better, drink better, take life-improving supplements, and exercise regularly. I also made a point of meditating daily and I did activities to strengthen my mental health further.

It's also important to be aware of who you are spending your time with, as they will influence who you become. As motivational speaker, Jim Rohn said, "You are the average of the five people you spend the most time with." This could be positive or negative depending on who you associate with, so choose your circle wisely.

Taking care of all these things led me to being the healthiest I'd ever been in my body, mind, and soul. Recurrent migraines disappeared, along with large patches of dermatitis eczema. I was no longer fatigued, anaemic, and iron deficient. Catching colds and viruses became a rarity. My allergies were reduced or cleared up. My gut health and digestion improved significantly. My skin glowed, and my hair and nails became stronger. I had so much energy and positive vitality. It was like being born again into a new body! And I loved it!

What happened next, I couldn't comprehend. My world got turned upside down. I was in shock. Life was never going to be the same again. I had to embrace a new change that I really wasn't prepared for.

My father unexpectedly passed away at age 62. One moment, Dad was out and about doing his usual things; the next moment—he was gone. My Dad hadn't been feeling well, and after visiting the doctor, they told him to visit A&E (Accident and Emergency). He went and was seen by the doctors there. They discharged him on the same day with a prescription to take. That evening at home, his breathing and heart failed. One of my family members found him, and they did what they could to revive him. An ambulance was called, and several paramedics came. After a long ordeal, they got his breathing and heart beating again, but Dad was still unconscious.

He was taken to A&E. The same A&E where he was earlier that day. Scans were taken and things were not looking good. His brain was so damaged by the lack of oxygen that he would never wake up or breathe without the ventilator. We had to come to terms with this new reality—no longer having Dad in our lives. In the early hours of the following morning, with my family and me around Dad's hospital bed, the priest said a prayer. We said goodbye to Dad, and the machine was turned off. Dad breathed on his own for a little while before passing away.

Driving to the hospital in my car to say goodbye to Dad in the early hours was like being in a horror movie. The streets were empty, quiet, and dead. There was not another soul in sight. The roads were misty and cold.

Driving back from the hospital after saying goodbye, I felt

numb. Daylight started to break. I still had businesses to run, and my 8-year-old child to take care of and tell him Granddad had gone. My mind was processing everything, trying to make sense of what had happened and why.

Dad was not the healthiest of people. Before his collapse, he had several health problems, including those with his heart and lungs, but he just got on with life and his day-to-day routines as best he could. He didn't eat or drink in the healthiest way or take care of his physical health as well as he could have. That was his choice and decision. It could also be said that the hospital didn't do enough to take care of Dad when he visited A&E that day. This experience strongly reinforced to me the importance of taking care of our well-being. Our overall health and happiness is so important, because without them, we truly have nothing. Alongside this, we must live life now. We can't assume or take for granted that there will be a tomorrow. Each day is a gift, and we must embrace it.

Following Dad's death, and this overwhelming feeling that we must live fully while we can, I was deeply inspired to create an online group as part of the health, wellness, and beauty business I was in to help improve the health of people's body, mind, and soul. Through this group, and with the help of some incredible people, I was able to help over 100 people improve their health, fitness, mindset, and spiritual connection. Many lives were permanently changed for the better. Including mine!

I had no idea that creating this group for others, and the journey that followed, would inspire me to become a certified life coach. Due to unforeseen changes within the health and wellness team and the business, I decided to create and build my own life coaching business. I am passionate about helping individuals to achieve their personal and professional goals whilst taking care of their well-being through Inspired Action. It is so important to live in alignment with who we really are, from our heart space and soul. When you do this, anything becomes possible, and you truly start to live life on your terms.

The impact of creating my life coaching business has been profound. After coaching with me, my clients come out a transformed person. Their lives become more abundant with the things they desire; they have a stronger mindset and a stronger, healthier body. They achieve and exceed their personal and professional goals. They are more connected to their true selves. It is truly a total life transformation for the better.

In this work, I know I have found my calling. It is no longer about me but helping others to become their best selves. My mission is to help raise human consciousness and abundance through change and transformation. Even during the most adverse times. As Robin S. Sharma stated, "Push yourself to do more and to experience more. Harness your energy to start expanding your dreams. Yes, expand your dreams. Don't accept a life of mediocrity when you hold such infinite potential within the fortress of your mind. Dare to tap into your greatness."

As of today, I am still successfully running my cleaning business alongside my life coaching business. I graduated in 2017 with a BSc Honours in Psychology with The Open University. I am now also a Certified NLP Practitioner. Communication with my son's father is the best and calmest it's ever been, and my son is doing really well. It really is possible to embrace change and adversity for a better life.

I hope this chapter has helped to inspire you; and know that even during adversity, life can be changed for the better, and you can do it on your own terms.

ABOUT THE AUTHOR

CHANTELLE LYNCH

Chantelle Lynch currently lives in London, England, with her 11-year-old son. She helps coaches, business owners, and professionals overcome life's obstacles and challenges — to get unstuck and achieve their goals. Her clients win and live life on their terms by improving their well-being of body, mind, and soul as they take consistent Inspired Action.

Chantelle is a Certified Life Coach, NLP Practitioner, and has a BSc (Hons) Psychology Degree with a focus in Counselling. Her career experience spans across a variety of fields: Corporate, Blue Chip and private companies, NHS Public Service, Network Marketing, Charities, and Volunteering. She has been a self-employed business owner since 2016 and absolutely loves it. Working with and coaching people to reach their personal and professional goals has been extremely rewarding.

Contact Information

Website: www.chantellelynchcoaching.com
Facebook: https://www.facebook.com/chantelle.lynch.142
Instagram: https://www.instagram.com/imchantellelynch

Chapter 11

Beauty Can Come from Brokenness

Rachel Hewitt

Looking back, I realised I should have listened to my mother...

Cling!

"Cheers to new beginnings!" We cheered as we marked the moment.

Our wedding day was one of the happiest moments of my life. All of the people who meant the world to me came to celebrate. I remember feeling so excited, and for probably the first time in my life—beautiful.

I had the most gorgeous ivory silk gown ordained with white flowers and pearls, which I had picked out with my mum. That day is still written through my heart. It had been a beautiful balmy summer Edinburgh day. I had booked an appointment with a beautiful bridal shop in town, and me, my mum, a family friend, and one of my bridesmaids all excitedly rang the doorbell. Giggling and champagne bubbles filled the air as we searched through the most beautiful dresses made of satin and silk. I selected three to try, and one by one I put them on and twirled in front of my chosen few.

When I put on the dress that would be mine, it felt like home, as though it had been made for me. So many people said I would know the right dress when I put it on, but I didn't believe them until that moment. Gasps and squeals came from my friends and mum. This was it. This was my dress. Dad came in, agreeing it was beautiful. This was the most precious gift my mum and dad had ever given me.

On the morning of the wedding, the florist arrived with a bouquet filled with cornflowers, white and pink roses, lily of the valley, shells, and sparkles. It was everything the little girl inside me had dreamed of.

The church was buzzing with excitement. A huge flower explosion hung in the rafters alongside numerous tissue pom-poms; we had spent the last few weeks making. I had two of my most cherished friends by my side. My wonderful father came to collect me, and I felt ready to set this new season into motion.

"Great, are you ready?" said the minister.

My heart was caught in my throat. I swallowed and exclaimed, "Yes!"

And that was it.

As the music began to play, my heart skipped down the aisle. There, gazing at me, was the one my heart loved—the one who had noticed me, cherished me. We exchanged vows with tears flowing from us both and spun our way back up the aisle to "Walking on Sunshine." We danced through the rest of our day, flying on newfound wings. To have and to hold from this day forth.

Beaches had been so special to me and this man while dating, so having a hotel that looked out onto the sea seemed only right for our reception. It was beautiful, and our dear friends and family danced and celebrated with us into the night.

We booked a little house up on the Isle of Skye for a week. It was a beautiful wooden house with a storm door. "You'll need that this weekend," said the owner. "There are 90 mph winds expected!"

We didn't mind too much though; there was a log fire, stunning scenery, and places to explore. We had saved up to eat at an award-winning Michelin Star restaurant nearby. This was such an amazing experience. After seeing the chef win a meal on *Great British Menu,* we couldn't wait to go and try it for ourselves. I remember being so excited as we entered the restaurant and sat down.

"Are you celebrating something special?" said the waiter

"It's our honeymoon," I replied, smiling at my new husband.

He was as cold and distant as could be. I wasn't sure what the matter was, but from the waiter's expression, I could see he had also found that something was not right. The whole meal I felt like I was eating alone, and though my heart tried to enjoy it, there was a sinking feeling in my stomach and a horrible pang in my gut. He hadn't really been himself since a conference we were at. Since that day, it had felt like everything I had hoped for and loved was unravelling in front of me. I had tried to knit it back together, but as I knitted, it unravelled.

"It is all going to be fine," I told myself. *"Just keep going."*

He had chased me—writing beautiful cards and letters, and chatting till the early hours. He had won my heart, and I couldn't let that slip away. This was real!

The day he proposed, we had planned a lovely picnic at La Caleta Beach. My heart was doing summersaults as I knew it was going to happen. That afternoon, I went to the pool with my mum. She sat next to me, and I knew there was something she wanted to share.

"Rachel," she said. "This man is going to propose tonight. Are you sure this is what you want?"

Mum and dad had come over for the week so that when we were engaged, we could all go out and celebrate as two families together.

"He hasn't been in a good place the last while. Are you sure you don't want to wait?"

The truth of these words cracked open a place I had been ignoring. There were signs that I should wait, that things weren't right. However, this was love; he loved me, we had fun—this is what I had dreamed of. I couldn't let this go.

"It's all going to be fine, mum," I said quickly, not allowing her words any deeper. "It has been hard, but it is all going to be okay.

I love him."

After all the adventures of the wedding and honeymoon, it arrived—day of departure. The day had been full of many façades of emotion. The man I married and I had been packing the rest of my life into what could fit into two 20-kg bags and carry-ons.

As we waved goodbye to family and friends, my heart was full of nervous, excited hope and love, and pricked with pain. In a shower of tears and confetti, I waved goodbye to family, home, and Scotland.

The airport came into sight; it was time to embark on all the new things that were waiting in this new season.

"Cheers to new beginnings!" We cheered on the plane as we cracked open some bubbly.

"Let's always celebrate these moments," I said.

Arriving at our destination, I was warmed by the sun's heat and the gentle soothing sound of the swifts. To me, it felt like their melody warmed the mix of emotions in my heart, as in a place of unknowingness, there was a sound familiar and kind. Waiting for us at Malaga was my new husband's best man with a sign saying *MR & MRS!* Hugs and laughs were exchanged. As he drove us to our first nest, we shared the stories of our wedding and honeymoon. We were staying in a lovely flat in Spain.

The next morning, I was greeted by warm, metallic air and

rays of sunlight seeping through the blinds. Time to explore! I loved walking into Gibraltar along the seafront, hearing the waves crash and smelling the warm, salty air.

Kindness in this place—which had been unloved and forgotten, and seen much pain and sadness—is like finding a diamond in a rubbish dump. On my daily walks, I found many diamonds hiding in unknown places. Yet I could feel the tension between the two places—Spain and Gibraltar.

In some ways, this echoed my new marriage. Tensions crept in. The more I tried to hold everything together, the more it broke in new places. Looking back now, I wasn't happy—my heart was breaking. I didn't know what happened, and, in some ways, still to this day I am none the wiser. All the happiness drained away that year in different ways. I was so full of fear I couldn't swallow, and all I wanted was to be happily married to a man I thought loved me and that I loved. Silent thoughts resonated. I had moved away from my whole life, my family, and everything I knew for this. It was then, looking back, that I realised I should have listened to my mother that day by the pool. I could have waited.

One day, a year later, on the bathroom floor, tears began to run. I remember my husband's coldness and angry words resonating through the house, his eyes so empty. My father had never spoken to me in that way. There was nothing I could do; I didn't know how to rescue him or us. This wasn't the first time, but it was the one I was most scared of. Clenching onto my hopes, I had to make this work. I believed in fighting for marriage. There must be a way. It seemed moving to Scotland might be a way to save things, so we went.

Thorn after thorn kept tearing our marriage apart. Again, I kept knitting as things unravelled, but by this time it seemed all hope was gone.

Eventually, through a painful conversation, the marriage ended.

Surges of pain like shards of ice, too big to handle, broke out, trapping me in the center, unable to breathe. I pushed the emotions down. The day my husband left literally tore my heart into pieces.

Six years later, I had a unique experience…

I looked through those shattered pieces lying around in the garden of my heart. I gently collected them together in my hands, recalling each moment, feeling their emotion. Then broken, I give them to Jesus. Placing them into His hands, my heart pounds at the thought of Him maybe being disappointed in me.

Breathing, I look up, my tear-sparkling eyes catching His gaze, and there, with glints of tears in his eyes, is a warm, welcoming kindness. "I'm glad you've come," He said tenderly.

As I searched deeper into His eyes, I suddenly noticed His heart, and there was the mirror echoing the broken pieces that were within mine. I realised then he had felt and walked every part as me, not just with me. He knew exactly how it felt. I wasn't alone in the pain; he was in the whirling torment of emotion with me.

I gasped, allowing the tears to flow.

He reaches out, holding me close. Weeping together, I allow all the pain to pour out to the ground around us. All my disappointment, broken hopes, and the words angrily spoken to me washed away. Jesus wasn't disappointed in me. I had fought with my whole heart for what I believed in. He was proud of me. Jesus's arms were reassuring and safe.

Tears created puddles, which created pools, and in the garden of my heart there was now a peaceful river flowing. Around the river, flowers started to bloom, trees budded, and there was a carpet of life flourishing from the ground. The tears quietly lessened, and the shards of pain which had become my daily companions were gone.

I sat with him on the grass next to the river. Peace now filled my heart. Jesus then held out his hand to me, and where the broken pieces had been, there was now a precious heart that looked like a diamond. Together, we placed it into my heart. There it shone, sang, and sparkled beautifully.

"Thank you," I whispered joyfully, tears filling up my eyes.

He smiled; laughter, joy, and hope beamed from His face. "I love you, my beloved."

I made many mistakes in those six years trying to find myself again, to soothe the brokenness. However, they just broke me more. Now facing the pain and walking through the healing, there is new hope glittering.

I stumbled across an old diary the other day. Reading through the prayers, tears, and promises of those few years of marriage (before we moved to Scotland), I found amongst the pages something so beautiful. I had drawn a picture where God had promised me to flourish in the future, turning my brokenness into a river where the banks would thrive and blossom with life. I had even drawn flowers with a river running through them on the page, the same as in my encounter with Jesus. I realised my healing had already been guaranteed and fulfilled before my heart had even fully broken.

He knows the beginning from the end in your life stories. Life isn't always how we dreamed it, but He promises to turn everything into something beautiful.

This chapter is dedicated to my unbiological sister, Antoinette. Thank you! I love that we can talk for hours about everything and nothing, have tea in a cafe for seven hours, we've wept, laughed till our stomachs ached, drunk cocktails till the early hours, and dissected our favourite TV shows. I know I wouldn't be where I am in life without you. We've walked the highs and lows of the journey of life together. Cheers to more adventures, sister!

"We're almost there and nowhere near it.
All that matters is that we're going!"
—Lorelai Gilmore, Gilmore Girls

ABOUT THE AUTHOR

RACHEL HEWITT

Rachel Hewitt is a dancer, artist, and wellness therapist. She loves seeing people flourish into wholeness through wellness and encounters with Jesus. Rachel also loves party planning and celebrating precious occasions with people and holds regular wellness retreats as part of her business. She loves dancing to cheesy music, seeing friends, long country walks, cosy cafes, art galleries, and the theatre! Plus, anything sparkly! Rachel won the Best Aromatherapy Blender Award in her year at college and received her Master's degree at Glasgow University.

Contact information can be found on the next page.

Contact Information

Email: Joysorganicdelight@gmail.com
Instagram: @Joysorganicdelight

Chapter 12

The Unexpected Path to Self-Discovery

Jennifer Lee

In a world where the familiar feels safer than the unknown, in a life where your comfort zone may conflict with your soul's purpose. With an inner world that believes you are who you are and will remain that way for life, and there is nothing you can do to change it.

If you fail to listen to your inner words, miss the external signs, and ignore your intuition and the negative feelings in your body, the universe might just step in to ensure you do what you came here to do. Life will hit you with a truck that warrants a redirection on your path, resulting in a new world of uncertainty, self-discovery, and healing. You'll be forced to dig deep into the unknown to uncover courage and embrace change, deliberately creating change.

You might ask yourself, "Why do I need to change?"

The next questions to ask are: "What will I lose if I don't change? And what will I gain if I do?"

My favourite quote by Mark Twain is, "Twenty years from now you will be more disappointed in the things you didn't do than by the ones you did do."

When I think back to the people I have met, they all seemed to have this one story that made an impact on their life, creating a massive redirection and trajectory of their lives. I would often feel like I didn't have one of those moments of impact that changed my life, changed my direction, or had a worthy story to share. Changes just happened to me incrementally, creating a massive impact on the direction of my life, which cannot be shared in a short chapter.

This story is about a girl on her way to Tomorrowland, the biggest dance festival in the world. This experience was the beginning of the biggest impact on her life, creating a redirection she could never have predicted.

The girl in this story is me.

I had planned a three-month trip: Global Journey to Tomorrowland, Berlin, Prague, United Kingdom, United States, Bahamas, Mexico, finishing off with a 4-day trek to Machu Picchu and down through South America. I planned the trip around Tomorrowland.

Unaware at the time, my trip was a way to escape my reality, to cover up the deep misery I was in, feeling out of control, created by multifaceted conflicted beliefs that were running on my old programming.

The journey begins in Hong Kong and then to Paris.

I had visited Paris twice before, so I decided to see the main attractions on the back of a scooter. The next morning, I awoke to a sore back, right in the centre where my spine is. Little did I know what was manifesting.

As the days went on, travelling from Amsterdam to Berlin, I found myself struggling emotionally, and my health seemed to decline. We arrived in Berlin to begin the Global Journey tour to Tomorrowland.

Instead of doing what I was there to do—party, dance, and experience the amazing Berlin nightclubs—all I wanted to do was crawl into a bed and sleep.

The next day, our first official day in Berlin, while sightseeing, I collapsed. My back felt like it was on fire. This day was a public holiday and no doctors were open, so I found my way to a hospital with the help of a friend.

When I got there, the nurse examined my back and said to me in a German accent, "The pus, we need to drain the pus!"

An ingrown hair was discovered.

"An ingrown hair on my back? How can I have an ingrown hair on my back? There is no hair on my back!?"

I laid on the hospital table, and without warning, I let out a scream. The nurse had attempted to squeeze, slapped a band-aid on it, and sent me on my way.

The next two days, I was determined not to miss out on the activities and pushed myself to enjoy it all. Whilst feeling drained and homesick, I put on my brave face.

On our last night in Berlin, true Jen-style, I partied, danced, and drank copious amounts of alcohol, forgetting I was exhausted.

Waking up around midday, in pain, hungover, and barely coherent, I discovered from the mirror's reflection that there was a blister the size of a fifty-cent piece appearing on my back now.

Revisiting the hospital, the same nurse looked me over. I waited and waited for a doctor only to be told that I would need surgery, as the hair needed to be surgically removed, and this could not be done while I was conscious.

I awoke feeling cold in a hospital bed. No pain at this stage; the drugs were keeping me happy and comfortable. The surgery was a success, and the ingrown hair had been removed, leaving me with a deep hole in my back, packed and covered.

The instructions my friend received were to clean it with water; no medications or antibiotics were prescribed. We left the hospital around midnight, knowing that we were scheduled to catch the crowded train to Prague at 7 a.m.

Arriving in Prague, I managed to find a home doctor who visited me in the hostel the day after arrival. She looked at the wound and advised that there wasn't anything she could do and that I needed to go to the hospital immediately. So, I went.

I laid on the hospital table. This time a surgeon examined me and said that the wound had become infected. It had now become an abscess. He informed me that the wound would need to be cleaned, and the infected skin would need to be scraped off. He applied a local anaesthetic. As he began to clean, I let out a very loud scream, and tears began to well up in my eyes.

The doctor, with empathy, apologised and said that the local anaesthetic was not enough to numb the area. He then went on to tell me there weren't any spare beds for surgery and asked would I agree to have it done now as it was.

All I wanted was for this nightmare to be over, so I agreed.

The only thing I had in that moment was a white quartz crystal that I had in my pocket (my spiritual healer had gifted it to me). It kind of became my security blanket.

A white quartz crystal can be used for healing purposes; benefits include stress relief and giving off a calm energy, which I didn't know at the time.

Traumatised by the moment, I held the crystal tightly in my hand. Tears flooded my eyes, rolling down my cheeks, screams followed without sound—the pain excruciating, as if my insides were being sliced open.

Once it was over, I took a deep breath and noticed my hand was left with deep imprints from the crystal.

This event repeated every day whilst in Prague, like the movie *Groundhog Day*.

Every day since my surgery was a fun trip to the hospital, fearing it would become infected again. I saw more hospitals in Europe than I have in Australia.

Despite my health being up and down, we arrived in Belgium by bus, where we exited the bus on the holy grounds of Tomorrowland.

That day, I checked-in to a hotel room with blackout blinds and a mattress that felt like a cloud. I slept for 12 hours.

The next day was Day 1 of Tomorrowland. I truly believed at that point I was still going.

Tomorrow arrived, and I began to slowly move around, feeling weak, tired, and afraid that someone would bump into my back.

As I made my way to the bathroom, I attempted to lift my leg over the side of the bath. Then I collapsed down onto the floor—naked, wailing, tears flowing like a river. Reality settled in—I was not going to experience Tomorrowland.

I booked myself a flight to Cardiff, Wales, where my extended family lives.

I arrived and was greeted by my cousin, who is a nurse. I spent the next 2 weeks being cared for by my cousins while

I rested and healed.

"What did I do to deserve this?" I wondered whilst lying in bed, trying to feel grateful that I was with family and not alone. Although I was self-sabotaging myself as I watched the live event on YouTube, I began asking out loud, "Why me? What did I do wrong?"

No answers, just silence.

Returning home, I hit a new rock bottom. Everything in my life was falling apart. I was faced with uncertainty in my job, separation, court, and divorce, and although my wound was healing, my health continued to decline. I was depressed, miserable, and still wondering why.

I began to get curious, especially the part where my body had manifested an ingrown hair without any hair on my back. Researching through various spiritual books, with the help of a friend who had begun her own healing journey just a few months earlier, using books that explained the causes of physical ailments stemming from emotional experiences and conditions.

Metaphysical Anatomy, written by Evette Rose, became my favourite book; it was like my bible. It's a book of psychosomatics. Essentially, the book helps you become aware of and understand the causes of emotional, mental, and physical ailments that stem from ancestry, conception, birth, and childhood.

An abscess, in a nutshell, is manifested by fermenting thoughts over hurts, slights, and revenge; and suppression of anger, rage, and resentment all trapped in the solar plexus area (where my abscess was located). I found this information throughout various books.

The Solar Plexus chakra is in the diaphragm area in the upper abdomen of the body. It is energetically linked with the eyes, pancreas, kidneys, and adrenals and associated with digestion and metabolism. Based on self-esteem, self-confidence, identity, and personal power. Often called "The Warrior" or "lustrous gem" chakra for the confidence, power, drive, and gleaming within that is felt when balanced, which I was clearly not.

I know what you're thinking: What the hell does that all mean?

It means that I had a long road ahead of me to discover just what that meant.

Soon after, I picked up a book that was recommended to me called *The Emotion Code*, written by Dr. Bradley Nelson. I learned how to communicate with my body using a form of kinesiology and began to release my trapped emotions of anger, rage, resentment, and 57 other unknown negative emotions that were festering in my body.

Every day I began to feel better and better, releasing at least 5–10 emotions a day.

At the publishing of this book, it has been 5 years since that traumatic and heartbreaking ordeal. That experience, however, redirected me on a healing journey, which is still ongoing. I became a lifelong learner into becoming a specialist of how the mind, body, soul, and spirit work together. Discovering that change can occur in an instant with the tools, techniques, and processes I have learnt since that day.

I've rewired my mind, changed many unwanted thoughts, behaviours, habits, resting emotional states, beliefs, negative internal stories, and programming. I have healed 99% of my health issues. I feel younger and healthier today than I did 5 years ago, and now when an imbalance occurs, I'm so connected to my body that I can sometimes resolve those triggers within seconds (this is not always the case, however).

A couple of weeks ago, my mum handed me a box. In it I found my biography book, which I wrote about myself when I was 12 years old. In Chapter 6, "My Character," I wrote: "I am a person who likes to help people that are in trouble."

And that is exactly what my life is all about—helping anyone in my life that needed or wanted my help in some way. This is now on a greater scale, specific and deliberately changing myself and helping people from all over the world improve their health and relationships at an accelerated rate.

I am and will be forever grateful for that traumatic experience that happened to me 5 years ago, as I've become a person that I never thought possible. Although I'm just like you—a work in progress. Every day is a new day to be better than the day before.

In the words of Tony Robbins, "Life is always happening for you, not to you."

Yes, it is.

As I say those words, my eyes begin to well up, sitting in a coffee shop at a crossroad, enduring another huge transition in my life—cultivating courage, embracing deliberate change.

I have faith that the Universe (or God, depending on your beliefs) has my back, redirecting me to my soul's purpose.

ABOUT THE AUTHOR

JENNIFER LEE

Jennifer Lee is a passionate advocate for personal growth and resilience, possessing extraordinary intuitive gifts that guide her in empowering others. With a knack for problem-solving and a humorous approach to life's challenges, she has dedicated her life to helping herself and individuals uncover their potential. Jennifer believes that every obstacle presents an opportunity for transformation, and she thrives on facilitating those breakthroughs. Her enthusiasm for health and fitness complements her holistic perspective on well-being, motivating those around her to embrace a balanced lifestyle. Known for her unwavering determination, Jennifer sets ambitious goals and chases them with relentless energy, inspiring others to pursue their dreams with the same fervor. An adventurous spirit, she loves exploring new experiences and dancing her heart out. A firm believer in the power of community, Jennifer is committed to creating spaces where individuals can connect, grow, and support one another in their quests

Contact information can be found on the next page.

Contact Information

Instagram: @jennifer.lee.official

Chapter 13

HIStory

Jay C. Denis

Trigger warning: Includes the details of a suicide attempt.

At 23 years old, I had it all—a nice little car and a motorbike too. I had a great job working as a personal trainer with wonderful clients. Most importantly, I had a loving and supportive family.

However, this would soon all change.

On the 23rd of December, we were at a friend's house and decided to go to the mall. We took two cars. Four of us jumped in my car plus another friend we picked up on the way. There was Dave, Mars, T, my little brother, and myself.

From there, we made our way to the mall. Both cars stopped at the lights. As we proceeded to take off, a different car passed me on the inside lane, then cut me off and jammed on their brakes. My initial reaction was to swerve to avoid hitting the other car. As I swerved, my car began to fishtail before going into a spin. We mounted the kerb and hit a light pole. The force of the impact caused the light pole to come crashing down, narrowly missing my car.

As the car came to a stop, Dave, who was the front seat passenger, leapt out of the car and ran off. I looked behind and noticed the left rear side of the vehicle had caved in. It was dark, and I couldn't see T, who was seated in the left rear seat; or Mars, who was seated in the middle.

To this day, a memory that I will never forget is seeing my brother. His eyes, white and wide open, stared right back at me.

I asked him, "Are you okay?"

He replied, "I can't move. I can't feel my legs."

I exited my car and realised I had sustained a foot injury. I tried to open the rear door where my brother was, but it was stuck.

My other friends in the lead car soon realised we were no longer following them. They turned around and came back for us.

I sat next to the car. We soon heard emergency sirens. To extract my brother, the fire brigade used the jaws of life. Once they removed the roof of the car, I heard them say, "The guy in the middle is dead."

They tended to my brother and managed to remove him from the wreck safely and carefully. At this point he had begun to bleed from the ear, which often can be a sign of brain damage.

T had sustained significant facial injuries, and 15 minutes later, she was also pronounced dead.

My other friends were able to locate Dave, and as the ambulances arrived, my brother was first taken away, followed by Dave, and then myself.

When Dad arrived home, he received a call from emergency services informing him there had been an accident and their youngest son had been taken to Alfred Hospital. They didn't know my condition or whereabouts. In a panicked state, he had completely forgotten how to get there. So, he called my uncle, and he and my mum went to their place before making their way to the hospital.

It wasn't until they arrived at the hospital that they realised I was alive and ok, along with my little brother and Dave. However, tragically, two of our friends had died in the accident. My brother had sustained a neck injury and had to wear a neck brace. (Thankfully, no brain damage.) Dave had a small bone fracture in his hand. I only sustained a small cut to my right foot.

Dave and I were released from the hospital the following day, while my brother was released on Christmas Day. Christmas was a non-event that year. In the coming days, we would have to bury two of our friends.

I went back to work in the new year and had a couple of counselling sessions. I even bought another car.

It wasn't until April that Dave, my brother, and I were all contacted by the police to come in and make a report. A few weeks later, I was charged with numerous driving offences related to the accident. The most serious being dangerous driving, which carried a maximum penalty of two years imprisonment.

The case went through the courts for nearly a year, at which point a few of the charges were dropped. However, a couple of charges remained.

On the final day of the case, I remember this as one of the loneliest days of my life. I sat up on the front bench all alone. Knowing I had driven myself to court, had come in via the front entrance, and there was a chance that I could be leaving from another entrance and heading off to prison. However, the judge was very reasonable. I had a clean driving record, this was my first accident, and my family and I have no criminal records. We were made an offer, which included a loss of license for 3 years, community service, and a fine. My lawyer, my family, and I deliberated on the decision. Our lawyer mentioned that it was a good outcome if the verdict you are given is anything but jail. Consequently, we ended up taking the deal.

So, life went on, but I felt guilty to an extent for having taken the deal. Not a day went by when I didn't think about the accident, my friends, or what I was doing with my life. What if I had done things differently? Could I have avoided that accident? Maybe I should have just stayed home that night. These feelings of blame, helplessness, and hopelessness went on for many years.

I decided to go back to university to further educate myself —a distraction, a focus. Something to help occupy my mind and my time.

During this time, I also met the woman of my dreams. She was smart, beautiful, aspirational, career-minded, and very independent. Six months later, we moved in together. The following year, we purchased a new home together. We then decided that we should get married and started to plan our wedding.

However, it was around this time that I was becoming more anxious about everything—the wedding, the house, the accident, and my university studies.

I wasn't enjoying things like I used to. I was becoming more withdrawn. I had stopped training and going to the gym, stopped listening to music, and even stopped playing golf, which I loved playing with friends on the weekends. I was skipping university. Consequently, my grades started to fall. I felt like I was letting my classmates down. Most of all, I felt as though I was letting my family and my partner down. Maybe I wasn't good enough for her.

I hadn't slept much in the preceding days and weeks. On the morning of the 23rd of May, I waited for my partner to go to work. Once she left, I got up and went downstairs. I was a mess and began thinking all sorts of crazy thoughts. I was meant to go in to work that day, as well as prepare for a presentation at university. I called in sick to work and then started to ignore calls from my university friends. I jumped online and tried contacting mental health services. I even called a mental health service provider but was put on hold for well over 30 minutes. At this point in time, I thought, "Yep, this is it! I'm SUICIDAL!"

I felt like a massive letdown to everyone. So, I thought about ways to kill myself. I drove down to the local supermarket, purchased a packet of razor blades, returned home, and sat on the back deck.

I started slicing a large incision on my right arm, from my wrist to my elbow. Unsatisfied, I added another. There's blood everywhere, but not enough. It was the middle of winter in Melbourne, and maybe the cold kept me from bleeding out? I switched sides, adding similar cuts to my left arm. I then started slicing deeper into the cuts I had already made with the intention of bleeding to death. However, the cold weather seems to have stemmed my bleeding.

I then went inside the house and started filling up the bathtub with hot water, thinking if I can get warm again, the blood may start flowing. So, I jumped into the bathtub and continued cutting. There were chunks of flesh and exposed muscle from my wounds, but again I stopped bleeding.

Desperate, I took my partner's hair dryer and straightener from the bathroom basin. I turned them on and threw them in the tub with me, but our modern tub prevented me from electrocuting myself to death. I even submerged myself underwater, holding the straightener and hairdryer to my chest, feeling the electricity pulsate through me. But all to no avail. After minutes submerged underwater, I sat up and said, "I'm not going to fucking die today, am I?"

At this point, maybe I'm just not meant to die. However, I'm still intent on dying. I get up, get dressed, and phone the police. It's my hope that they will shoot me dead if they see me armed with knives. But it's not fair—the guilt of killing me might haunt them forever.

I dropped the knives and walked outside. Removing my jumper, I showed them the wounds on my arms, and an ambulance was called. My partner is called as I'm taken to the hospital, and she calls my dad and brother while she races over.

Once admitted to the hospital, my wounds are assessed. I'm then prepped for surgery to get both of my arms stitched up. After the surgery, I finally got to see my partner, my parents, and my brother. It is evening now, and it has been an exhausting day for all.

My partner does not want to go back home for fear of what she will see and find. My dad and my brother go to our house to fetch her some belongings and begin to clean up. All the while, there's a mental health nurse by my side. Her role is to keep an eye on me.

Early the following morning, everyone was back at the hospital. I could see my parents, my partner, and my brother talking to what I assumed were psychiatric doctors. Would I go to a psychiatric hospital or go home?

I was determined to turn my life around and change because I knew life had much more in store for me. My two near-death experiences were a catalyst to help others afflicted by mental health illnesses, depression, and suicidal thoughts and tendencies. I could use this to motivate, educate, empower, and inspire people. At this point, without realising it, I had already started using the Neuro Linguistic Programming (NLP) technique of reframing. Simply put, reframing is a technique that changes the way we perceive an event and how this event is viewed.

When I finally left the hospital, I was heavily dependent on my partner. I attended counselling sessions as well as osteotherapy sessions to help strengthen my arms again.

With my rejuvenated passion and zest for life, I wanted to make a difference and work with people afflicted by mental health illnesses, depression, and suicide.

In the following years, I went back to university and completed my degree, majoring in nutrition and physical activity & health. Areas, which research has proven are integral to improving and maintaining optimal mental and physical health. I also obtained certifications in NLP, which complemented my boxing, personal training, and coaching qualifications and sessions. Hence, my coaching sessions not only focus on the physical aspect of boxing and learning a new skill but also incorporate breathwork, music, meditation, goal setting, and other elements of NLP.

I also got married, had a wonderful honeymoon in the Cook Islands, and most importantly, we were blessed with a beautiful baby daughter a year later.

Through everything that happened, what remained constant was the love and support that I had from my family and friends. Having a great support network is integral to coping with a mental illness. As a movie buff, I love Marvel movies, and one of my favourite movies is *Fantastic Four*. So, find your *Fantastic Four,* your four superheroes. Four people that can help motivate, educate, empower, and inspire you. Help keep you accountable. People you can depend on. That might be your parents, your partner, your friends, or even a coach or mentor like me.

At some point, we're all going to face challenges. However, challenge builds character, resilience, and determination. With a positive mindset and support network, we can achieve anything and help make a difference.

Often when people ask me: "Would you change anything?"

Now, I proudly say, "No."

I wouldn't be where I am today or the person I am today if it weren't for the challenges I faced. The challenges helped shape who I am, gave me purpose, and increased my desire to help people and help make a difference.

Hence, my business and support network is called PRIDE Health and Wellness. PRIDE stands for Purpose, Respect, Integrity, Dedication, and Education, and my motto is, "Take PRIDE in everything YOU do!"

ABOUT THE AUTHOR

JAY C. DENIS

Jay C. Denis is a successful and well-respected boxing coach, health and wellness advocate, Neuro Linguistics Practitioner (NLP), and an all-round nice guy! With qualifications in boxing, personal training, a degree in Health Sciences from Deakin University, and NLP certifications, Jay embraces the "healthy mind, healthy body" philosophy by incorporating elements of physical exercise, NLP/psychology, breathwork, and meditation to achieve amazing results.

A dedicated husband, doting father, dog dad, and weekend golfer, Jay's ultimate ambition is to help make a difference and give back—especially in the lives of those afflicted by mental health illnesses, depression, and suicide. He believes that through his business and support network called PRIDE Health and Wellness, he can positively impact the lives of others and provide help for those in need.

Contact Information

Phone number: +61 402 231 980
Email: jaycdenis@gmail.com
Email alt: jay@pridehealthandwellness.com.au
Website: pridehealthandwellness.com.au (under construction)
Facebook: Jay C Denis
Instagram: @jaycdenis26

Chapter 14

Building Unwavering Self-Belief

Stephanie Sullivan

In my late 40s, I have only recently come to the realisation that something is quite unique about me. Having coached professional women for a few years now, I have only recently realised how fortunate I am to lack the negative self-talk and self-doubt which many high-achieving professional women experience at some point in their career, if not regularly. In fact, a recent study by KPMG[1] found that as much as 75% of executive women experience imposter syndrome in their career or workplace. I was shocked it is this common, and that only 11% of executive women surveyed do not experience imposter syndrome or feeling unworthy or incapable.

In a quest aimed to help other women, as well as to fulfill my own personal curiosity, I have embarked on an exploration of self-discovery to unpack why or how I have escaped this trap of self-doubt and negative self-talk which plagues so many high-achieving, successful women. As mentioned, these women are successful! And many convey confidence to those around them, but it's that inner voice that questions her and holds her back.

According to KPMG's research study, the root causes of impostersyndrome "vary and may stem from childhood and school

---

[1] "Advancing the Future of Women in Business: A KPMG Women's Leadership Summit Report," 2020

experiences, familial expectations, societal stereotypes, cultural differences, and more." So, clearly there are a lot of things throughout our lifetime which can contribute to forming self-doubt and negative self-talk, but what is it that creates unwavering self-belief and the courage to step into unchartered territory?

Looking back at my childhood, I certainly did not grow up in a privileged (financially well-off) or even financially stable household. As long back as I can remember, my dad was self-employed in various businesses (he's a "jack of all trades"), and my mum was a full-time "stay-at-home mom" most of our lives, or sometimes running a Montessori school when we were very young.

As we progressed through school, we were limited in what sports and activities we could participate in due to the money required for uniforms, shoes, travel, and meals. But at the same time, my parents always seemed to find a way to support us when there was something we really wanted to do. They supported us in our interests, win or lose, good or bad performance. Going to the "big city" was a big deal, although we mostly shopped for our clothes at second-hand stores. I remember feeling privileged because we got the government-subsidised "free lunch" program at school (like how cool it was we got our lunch for free!) At some exceptionally tough times, my family even struggled to put food on the table and had to rely on a charity from the church. Many would probably think that my childhood did not set me up for success. But thankfully, that which my parents lacked in finances, they made up for in spades elsewhere.

Having our lifestyle, it would have been understandable for them to be negative, even hate the world and think it was unfair, or to stifle our expectations and ambitions to protect us from potential disappointment. Yet instead, they instilled this belief in us (me and my siblings) that we could accomplish anything we wanted or could dream of. They emphasised the importance of getting a good education (the best possible) and going after things we wanted with a strong determination and work ethic. We also knew that it was okay to reach for something and fall a little short, or even to lose or fail. At least we had tried. Acceptance and encouragement were at the core heart of our family and home.

Reminiscing about childhood with my brother recently, he said, "Poverty is a state of mind, and I never felt poor." In a similar sentiment, I also feel very privileged for my upbringing, despite it lacking the classical societal definition of being "privileged." I personally know other children, now adults, who grew up in similar financial circumstances to ours but lacked encouragement from their parents to strive for more. They were instead told not to desire for more than they had. We were thankful for what we had, but we also knew we could aspire for more. So, the key things my parents instilled in us were ambition, belief, and achieving.

However, we know from research, and from my personal observations as well, that many ambitious and even high-achieving people still battle with self-doubt and imposter syndrome. Having ambition and having self-belief are two very different things. Ambition is wanting to achieve something, whereas self-belief is knowing that you can achieve it. And while my parents also told us that we were very smart, capable, and beautiful people (inside and out), hearing it is also different than really truly believing it.

From my experience coaching many clients over the past few years, I understand that sadly not everyone grows up with this positive encouragement, and I am conscious and empathetic that you may likely fall into that camp, remembering and even replaying what you heard growing up as negative self-talk to this day. Maybe you were even told or made to feel that you are not smart enough, good enough, won't amount to anything or be successful. If so, here is the good news. As an adult, the person who has the most control of the narrative between your brain, lips, and ears is you! You have the power to change that narrative from negative to positive through practice and repetition.

I have seen my clients make significant improvements in their confidence and self-belief through reciting their core strengths along with affirmations such as: "I am deserving" or "I can do this!" or "I am good at my job!" We need to say it and hear it again and again to reprogram it as our default self-talk and self-belief. Only a few minutes a day can make a big difference.

To build self-confidence and self-belief, we also need evidence, and evidence comes from experience. Dr. Julie Smart talks about this in her book *Why Has Nobody Told Me This Before?* In her words, "Your brain learns like a scientist. Each time it has an experience, positive or negative, it clocks that as evidence for its beliefs." Like Dr. Smart, I also believe in the importance of building a bank of evidence that we can do things.

This brings me to another key part of my life which helped create unwavering self-belief and squash self-doubt. At the age of 23, I joined one of the "big 4" international consultancies. I thought I knew what I was signing up for, but I quickly learned that I didn't. Having just freshly completed my MBA, I thought I would be leveraging that knowledge to help companies with sexy things like business and marketing strategies (things which I was interested in and good at doing). Instead, in one of my early-on projects, I was expected to do computer programming to help build and test a system to be used by the largest telecommunication companies in the USA. Believe me, I virtually begged to get out of doing this.

My fear of failure was high, and I was young and just newly starting out in my career. I even divulged to my manager, "Trust me, you really don't want ME doing this. I failed computer programming in university, and because it was required to complete my math degree, I had to retake it during the summer holiday break, and I barely passed it the second time. I'm not the person you want doing this."

But guess what? He believed I could do it. I lost the argument and was thrown into a team of people who had computer science degrees and programming experience under their belts. I was dreading the task ahead of me, and the potential consequences of failure. In the end, I was shocked when my manager showed me that the code I created had the lowest defect rate of anyone on the team. Truly shocked! And don't ask me how.

I share this not to brag about my computer programming skills, as thankfully I left that pursuit behind ages ago. Rather, I share this story because of the valuable lesson(s) that it taught me early in my career. The only way to discover if you are good at something is to do it! And don't assume defeat or failure before you even try. And look, I even had strong historical evidence that I may struggle or fail. But every time I did it, I got a bit better at it. And, if I had never tried again, the only piece of evidence that would have remained in my belief system was that I couldn't do it. One big difference this second time around was that I had the support and belief of others backing me up, instead of a shitty professor who seemed to have a personal vendetta against me and was content, if not happy, to see me fail. When others show their belief in you, it's time to stand up and show belief in yourself!

However, it takes more than one piece of evidence to build unwavering self-belief. And for this, I have my 17-year consulting career to thank. For those who may not be familiar with consulting, it is a continuation of new project after new project every few months with different companies, industries, topics, cities, countries, bosses, clients, personalities, etc.. I was constantly thrown into situations which were new, ambiguous, and outside of my comfort zone. On many occasions, I didn't have prior experience, or even a clue about what I was being asked to do, and sometimes I was even positioned to clients as experienced or an expert in those areas. How do we respond in situations like this? Typically I would smile and nod in the client meeting, then have a quick "Oh shit!" moment before jumping into action. In my mind, there was no other option. Find a way or find another job.

When it came to something I didn't know, being curious and resourceful was key! I would consider the following: Who does know this or has done this before? What can I learn or reuse from their experience? What similar or relevant experience do I have that could be useful? Who else do I need to get involved to help?

A big part of imposter syndrome is the pressure and expectation we put on ourselves that we need to know everything, or how to do everything, combined with fear that we may be exposed as unknowing or inexperienced. A key step to overcoming this is to accept that there will always be things that we do not know, and new situations we have not previously encountered. It is impossible to have prior knowledge or experience in everything. This is just not realistic, in fact, it's an unreasonable expectation to place upon ourselves.

Instead, we can leverage our curiosity and resourcefulness to learn new things, and celebrate our learnings and growth. Trying something different or new may feel a little bit scary, especially when you're unsure of your ability to do it well. However, courage is taking a step forward in these moments, despite some uncertainty and fear.

In my view, the key difference between confidence and courage is action! You can be confident (believe you can do it), but not be taking action. Whereas courage is doing it — taking action, stepping outside of your comfort zone, and into unfamiliar territory. In experimenting with doing new and unfamiliar things, start small and work up to bigger challenges. Doing these things over time is what builds confidence and self-belief. The more you do things outside of your comfort zone, the more you grow and build stronger evidence and belief that you can.

As a business consultant, and even now as a professional coach, do you think that I have prior experience and knowledge about every possible situation that a client could raise to me? Of course not. The imposter tries to maintain the façade that we know, whereas the person of integrity and courage drops the mask and reveals that they don't know and solicits help from others. In situations where I find myself out of my depth of experience, I know (and sometimes need to remind myself) that I am resourceful and confident in my ability to support my clients in their needs, whether that involves expanding my knowledge on a new topic or bringing in someone else to help bridge a knowledge or skill gap. There is nothing wrong with that. In fact, it's a key vehicle for developing personal learning, growth, and unwavering self-belief.

Our lack of experience and even our prior failures do not dictate or determine our future success. You have the power to change your narrative (self-talk) from the reasons you can't, to the reasons you can. Confidence is believing you can, then courage is taking action! The more you step outside of your comfort zone to do new things, the more you build evidence (and self-trust) that you can, and the more comfortable it will become. As John Shedd said, "A ship in a harbor is safe, but that's not why ships are built."

ABOUT THE AUTHOR

STEPHANIE SULLIVAN

Stephanie Sullivan is a certified Life Coach, Health Coach, NLP Practitioner, member of the Global Coaching Association (GCA), and founder of Elevate Your Life Coaching PTY LTD.

After 25+ years in demanding, high-stress corporate roles as a business consultant, then a corporate executive, she knows first-hand about stress and trying to balance career and parenting demands, along with personal needs and wellbeing. This invaluable, real-life experience enables her to bring a realistic and pragmatic approach to coaching.

Stephanie helps business executives and professionals to boost self-confidence, courage, and personal wellbeing. She is passionate about performing her best at work and home without reaching burnout or constantly sacrificing one for the other.

Contact Information

Website: www.elevateyourlifecoaching.com.au
Email: steph@elevateyourlifecoaching.com.au
Linked-In: https://www.linkedin.com/in/stephanie-a-sullivan/
https://www.linkedin.com/company/elevate-your-life-coaching/
Facebook: https://www.facebook.com/profile.php?id=100066764244415

Epilogue

Jai Cornell

In every chapter, we see our coauthors generate the courage they need to make a change in their lives. Some made the decision on their own to change, while others were forced to make a change. Regardless of the circumstance, change is vital to growth and development. Without change, we would remain trapped in the same spot, our lives repeating while time continues to pass us by. How can that be considered living?

Dear reader, I ask that you examine the stories that you have just read. I ask that you feel the message that each coauthor poured their heart and soul into. None have told their story just to be a story. Every coauthor has shared a vulnerable moment of their past or thoughts they never let others hear in the hopes that their words would reach someone who finds themselves in a similar situation or perhaps to spare someone from getting into these situations.

So often, we wait until we have reached our lowest before we make a change. The fear of being anything but what we have known is scary—to leave our comfort zone we have known for so long. But when you take a step back, you will realize that your life has been full of change. From learning to walk and read, attending school and getting your first job, becoming a sibling or parent, getting your first car or learning to ride a bike—there were so many moments before now that required us to change, to adapt.

In moments where you feel like you cannot change because you are too afraid, just remember there were many times before this when you made astronomical changes—changes that were life-altering! You would not be who you are today without trying new things. You gathered up your courage and pushed forward, embracing change as you adapted. You did it once; you can do it again, and again, and again!

With a little bit of courage, you can do anything!

Thank you for choosing to read
Permission to Flourish: Cultivating Courage, Embracing Change

Made in the USA
Middletown, DE
26 November 2024